Streets

A Memoir of the Lower East Side

Bella Spewack

Introduction by Ruth Limmer
Afterword by Lois Raeder Elias

The Feminist Press
at The City University of New York
New York

Published 1995 by The Feminist Press at The City University of New York, The
Graduate Center, 365 Fifth Avenue, New York, NY 10016
First paperback edition 1996
Streets was first serialized in *Tenement Times,* a publication of the Lower East Side
Tenement Museum.

Library of Congress Cataloging-in-Publication Data

Spewack, Bella Cohen, 1899–1990
Streets : a memoir of the Lower East Side / Bella Spewack ; introduction by Ruth
Limmer ; afterword by Lois Elias.
    p. cm.
    ISBN 1-55861-115-0 (cloth : alk. paper)
    1. Spewack, Bella Cohen, 1899–1990—Homes and haunts—New York (N.Y.)
2. Lower East Side (New York, N.Y.)—Social life and customs.
3. Women dramatists, American—20th century—Biography. 4. Spewack, Bella
Cohen, 1899–1990—Childhood and youth. 5. Jews—New York (N.Y.)—Social
life and customs. I. Title.
    PS3537.P54Z475 1995
    812'.52—dc20
    [B]   95-13874
                                                        CIP

*This publication is made possible, in part, by public funds from the New York State
Council on the Arts and the National Endowment for the Arts, and by a grant
from the John D. and Catherine T. MacArthur Foundation. The Feminist Press is
also grateful to Joanne Markell and Genevieve Vaughan for their generosity.*

*Steven H. Scheuer, in memory of his mother, and in celebration of her life and
the 100th anniversary of her birth, is pleased to announce a substantial gift to
The Feminist Press to endow the Helen Rose Scheuer Jewish Women's Series.*
Streets *is the first named book in this series.*

Cover photo: Bella Cohen Spewack, 1921. Courtesy of the Samuel and Bella
Spewack Papers, Rare Book and Manuscript Library, Butler Library, Columbia
University.

For street scene photos, see pp. xxxv–xxxvii.

Interior design: Tina R. Malaney

Cover design: Ascienzo Design

Printed in the United States of America on acid-free paper by McNaughton &
Gunn, Inc., Saline, Michigan.

07 06 05 04 03 02 01 00   5 4 3 2

Contents

Publisher's Note

The Feminist Press is grateful to Arthur Elias, the executor of the Bella Spewack Estate, and Lois Elias for bringing the manuscript of *Streets* to our attention, and to Ruth Limmer, who suggested our name to the Eliases. Ruth Limmer also believed in the project enough to see that it was serialized (1994–95) in the *Tenement Times,* a publication she edits for the Lower East Side Tenement Museum. She did the initial copy-editing expertly and with utmost care for the author's own style; supplied explanatory footnotes where needed; and assisted us in obtaining reproducible prints of seven of the photographs included here.

We also thank the Rare Book and Manuscript Library at Columbia University (the home of the Sam and Bella Spewack Papers) and the New York Public Library photo archives for their cooperation on this project.

In the memoir, those footnotes followed by "R.L." were supplied by Ruth Limmer; those followed by "B.S." appeared in the original manuscript.

Introduction

Ruth Limmer

B ella Spewack was twenty-three years old, a tiny woman—in 1922 she would still have been called a "girl"—newly married and leaping with ambition. That her formal education had ended when she was graduated from Washington Irving High School in New York City made no matter. She had worked as a reporter, and she had already written and published a number of short stories. Now she and her husband, Sam, were foreign correspondents alternating between Berlin and Moscow. Now she would tackle the kind of extended narrative expected of a *real* writer—none of this journalistic "junk" as she called it. She would attempt a memoir.

She would ". . . pry open my coffin of memories" and describe her early life, beginning with her arrival on the Lower East Side in 1902 or 1903.

Her mother was an abandoned wife, at least that's how Bella described her. Whatever her true status, single parenthood could not have been comfortable in Transylvania. With Bella toddling alongside, the teen-aged Fanny Cohen left her family behind in the backwaters of the Austro-Hungarian Empire and came to America.

Tiny Bella would become famous. As a playwright and scriptwriter with her husband-collaborator Sam, she would hobnob with great artists and composers, would be the toast of Hollywood and Broadway. But first, Bella would have to learn English, endure the degradations of both poverty and charity, get an education, suffer loss of a beloved brother, and fight her way out of the Lower East Side.

Only learning English was easy.

Streets is the story of the hardships.

Streets is also the story Bella Spewack never submitted for publication. During her later years, she often talked about publishing the manuscript, but it was only talk. Did she fear that a commercial publisher would reject it? Did she want to maintain control over what the flap copy would say and how the book would be advertised? Her executor, the painter Arthur Elias, and his wife, media specialist Lois Elias, do not know to this day. But if it was fear of rejection, it was one of the very few times the adult Bella Spewack experienced fear.

As a professional, Bella Spewack understood that a writer had to put herself on the line. Sink or swim, when the curtain came down you either had a hit or you hadn't. The next day, one way or the other, you went back to the typewriter and began anew.

Because beyond being devastatingly witty, Bella was tough. She never pulled her punches, not in *Streets,* not in life. She spared neither herself nor anyone else. And she was painfully direct. When, as a child, a little boy pinched her, she did not go sobbing to the teacher. She kicked him, hard. How else would she have climbed out of those streets?

She began the ascent early. As her memoir details, she entertained others, she read, she explored, she examined her surroundings ruthlessly, and she began to write. Her first published piece appeared in the *Courier* of P.S. 147. In it, she took a dim view of the "little suffragettes" voting in the school election.

Then or earlier, she committed herself to becoming a writer. She was editor of her high school magazine. Once graduated, she sought jobs with newspapers. Bella could have attended college had she really wanted to. Hunter College was tuition-free and textbooks were supplied. Many girls combined work with higher education, even those like Bella who were partially responsible for the support of their families. But in fact high school was more education than most of Bella's generation received. Its full if rigid curriculum, combined with her passion for reading, provided the intellectual underpinnings of a career as a full-time professional writer. Her ambition and her desire to prove herself provided the rest.

But it was not easy to find newspaper employment. With some bitterness, she would tell about the managing editor at United Press International (UPI) who responded to her request for a job with a pat on the head and the comment, "We don't hire girls."

The Socialist paper *The Call* did employ "girls." For a handsome fifteen dollars a week Bella wrote for them under the name "Pippa." (In those years, every high school student knew Browning's poem in which the lark was on the wing and all was right with the world. But only a future writer of comedies would have adopted its name.)

By the time she married—it was March 17, 1922, and he was Sam Spewack, a handsome newspaperman from Staten Island with three years at Columbia University under his belt—she was a practiced reporter and the author of a number of short stories, published in both class and pulp magazines. While making her way, she was without snobbishness: *Redbook* and *The Freeman* were as good as MacFadden's *Fiction-Lovers Magazine*. They all paid, but not enough. She turned to press-agenting to make up the slack.

It was typical of her that the jobs were profitable, both to the organizations and herself. In an interview for the Columbia University Oral History project, she said of her work for the

Society of Independent Artists: "I was taught my art by some very excellent teachers, namely John Sloan, Robert Henri, and George Bellows. And I think it was during that time that I bought my first picture, paying twenty-five cents a week."

About applying to become press agent for the Campfire Girls—an organization surely unknown to youngsters from the Lower East Side—she said in the same interview, "I thought Campfire Girls, from the title, must be the woods, must represent outdoors. So I went to Fourteenth Street and got myself an outfit comprising a green jersey suit, orange stockings, brown shoes, and an orange hat. It seemed to me that represented the fire and the woods."

Funny. Unselfconscious. Smart. So smart that as press agent for the Girl Scouts she invented what she referred to as "that heinous, heinous thing, the Girl Scout cookie."

With such activities behind her, Bella may well have found herself with time on her hands when she followed her new husband to Europe in 1922. He was covering a peace conference for the New York *World*. She was working for *The Call*. ("The marriage of the capitalist and socialist press," she called it.) How does a young woman like Bella Spewack use her free time? Help your husband. Write more short stories. Tackle a memoir. Nose out human interest stories, most notoriously the discovery of Anna Anderson, the woman who claimed to be Anastasia, Grand Duchess of all the Russias.

In a sudden passion for authenticity, the magazine for which she had written the Anastasia story wanted to know if Anderson were really, truly the only surviving child of the murdered Romanovs. Bella demurred. No, she couldn't swear to it, and she would not—not then, not ever—compromise the truth to sell a story. Instead, she sold the piece to the *New York Times* for a lesser sum.

But it must have rankled. Bella was very, very careful about money. She had been scarred by poverty and understood how it degraded and enslaved.

Yet what she couldn't spend on herself, she could give away: to scholarships for girls who required help in completing high school, to the founding of a sports center for the disabled in Ramat-Gan, Israel. The sophisticated co-author of such Hollywood successes as *The Cat and the Fiddle, Weekend at the Waldorf,* and *My Favorite Wife,* and creator, with a bow to Shakespeare's *Taming of the Shrew,* of the book for Broadway's Tony award-winning *Kiss Me, Kate,* was one and the same as the bitter author of *Streets.* Bella Spewack was never free of her past and never forgetful of the obligations her successes laid upon her.

Bella and Sam began to write plays in 1926. It was her idea. They went to Hollywood, thanks to a casual conversation on a New York street. They were schmoozing with the writer/director George Abbott. Were they at loose ends? Why not try Lotus Land.

They went, they conquered.

Then World War II intervened. Sam joined the Office of War Information where, among other things, he wrote and produced *World at War.* Later, he served as press attaché to Averell Harriman, then the United States Ambassador to the Soviet Union. Bella promoted the sale of war bonds and worked to rescue children from the war zones. At war's end, she was sent to Eastern Europe as a representative of the United Nations to report on refugee camps for its Relief and Rehabilitation Agency (UNRRA). Impassioned, she also broadcast her observations on the ABC radio network.

Nothing, it seemed, was beyond the bright-eyed woman who had contended with the streets of the Lower East Side. Indeed, the Eliases tell an exactly fitting story:

When she was in her early eighties, and Sam had long been dead—he died in 1971—they accompanied her on a trip to Orchard Street, heart of the pushcart market of her childhood. She who could afford Saks and Tiffany's wanted to buy a pocketbook. Suddenly, she vanished. In a panic, the Eliases searched for the frail old lady—in stores, down streets, around corners. No Bella.

Hours later, they found her at home, serenely sitting in her favorite chair in her big ("too big, too big") Fifty-seventh Street apartment. Why had she disappeared? Where had she gone? How did she get home?

With a sardonic smile, she explained, as if to two people from Mars, that the Lower East Side was her territory. No one needed to help her get around. A taxi? What on earth for? The buses and subways still ran.

For Bella Spewack, they stopped running when she reached the age of ninety-one. It was April 27, 1990. With her husband, she had lived in Berlin and Moscow. With him, she had conquered Broadway and had lived and triumphed in Hollywood. After Sam's death, she had traveled the world around to inspect productions of *Kiss Me, Kate*. Married and then widowed, she finally settled "uptown," across from Carnegie Hall. But in the way she lived her life and in the stories she chose to tell, she never left the Lower East Side very far behind.

In her own superb memoir, *Lost in Translation*, Eva Hoffman speaks of the "not wholly joyful phenomenon" of the "desperado drive that fuels" what she calls "immigrant energy."

> But I also understand how it happens that so many immigrant Horatio Algers overshoot themselves so unexpectedly as they move on their sped-up trajectories through several strata of society all the way to the top. . . . It takes the same bullish will to gain a foothold in some modest spot as to insist on entering some sacred inner sanctum, and that insistence, and ignorance, and obliviousness of the rules and social distinctions—not to speak of "your own place"—can land you anywhere at all. As a radically marginal person, you have two choices: to be intimidated by every situation, every social stratum, or to confront all of them with the same leveling vision, the same brash and stubborn spunk.[1]

When she wrote *Streets,* Bella Spewack had not yet reached the top. Perhaps the top would not have been possible had she not written of the bottom in this raw, grief-filled, yet not infrequently funny memoir which tells of what she lived, what she saw, what she would hold for a lifetime in her "coffin of memories."

Laying aside its value as documentary history, Streets should serve as proof to new generations of immigrants that no social stigma can stand in the way of "desperado drive." It is time for it to be published.

But there is another way to view *Streets* and its author. While the memoir is, of course, unique—a personal document telling of the early experiences of one remarkable woman, it can also be read generically, as representative history of immigrant women who found themselves in urban America at almost any time between 1848 and 1915.

Clearly, Bella Spewack was extraordinarily gifted and adventurous. Nevertheless, what she lived through was in no way unusual. However harsh, however painful, her experiences were the stuff of urban immigrant life during the decades that marked the greatest influx of peoples into America that had ever been known. Even today, when immigration has again reached an all-time high, those decades remain exceptional in that they marked specifically European immigration—before 1880, most massively from Germany and Ireland; after 1880, largely from Eastern Europe and Italy.

In particular, Bella and her mother can be viewed as but two more Jewish females in a mass movement that ended on the eve of World War I. Over three and a half decades, well over a million and a half Jews from Eastern Europe joined approximately 80,000 mainly German Jews who had already found domicile in the United States.

A push-pull theory explains the flight of people from one country to another. Conditions at home grow increasingly severe; that's the push. Promise of a better life in the host country is the pull.

For the Jews from Eastern Europe—from which Bella and her mother came—the push was neither a failed revolution, such as the Germans fled after 1848, nor a potato famine such as the Irish fled after 1849, nor was it poverty and a growing absence of productive land that so many Italians faced at the turn of the century. Jews left because military conscription meant as many as twenty-six years in the Czar's army for the sons; because pogroms—government-sanctioned persecution—meant terror, and too often death, for an entire family; because the Enlightenment movement loosened religious bonds and made limited access to secular education a cause for aggrievement. As for Bella's mother, an equally compelling reason must have been that life as a single parent offered discomfort in a community shaped by religious observance in the cohesion of families.

The pull for all immigrants, including those from the Caribbean in the early part of this century, was the infinite promise of America, the Jews' *Goldene Medinah,* the Golden Land—the Chinese Golden Mountain—where anything was possible if you worked hard enough.

But what poor immigrants found, on the Lower East Side and elsewhere across the United States, was poverty. No matter what language they spoke, or what color their skins, if they were poor when they left, they were poor when they arrived. The streets were not lined with gold, actual or metaphoric.

Its absence is no surprise to us. But it was to them in the sense that for immigrants, no matter where they came from, New York was unimaginably foreign: harsh, treeless, disease-ridden, and bewildering. Even so, it was the land of no return for the Jews among them.

Other immigrant groups could dream of earning enough money in America to allow a prosperous return to a beloved homeland. Numbers of Italians happily accomplished this goal. For Jews, however, homelands were at best unfriendly, at worst murderous. For that matter, the United States wasn't crazy about them either. (It was not until the facts of the Holocaust became common knowledge after World War II that overt anti-Semitism finally became reprehensible.)

For courage, the immigrants banded together and began the long climb out of wretchedness. Germans, generally the best educated and least needy of nineteenth-century immigrants to the Lower East Side, rolled cigars and opened shops. The Irish and Italians, among the least educated, worked as laborers; there were bridges and roads to build, subway tunnels to excavate, buildings to erect. And because most had English, public employment—especially with the police department—soon opened for Irishmen. Irish women, who frequently arrived alone and unmarried, went into domestic service. Italian women, who came with their men, most often worked at home, making artificial flowers or lace for the gentry. Their liberated daughters would get the rare privilege of working outside the home; they got to slave over sewing machines for the garment industry. Jews, men and women alike, peddled and plied needles.

But grouping together in enclaves that came to carry labels like Kleindeutschland (Little Germany), Chinatown, and Little Italy had a downside. As more and more immigrants arrived to share language, solace, and houses of worship with their compatriots, their neighborhoods grew increasingly crowded. Density led to visibility. Visibility gave birth, within the host population, to nativism. So widespread was it that in its least egregious form, anti-immigrant feeling might even express itself in popular song. A well-known entertainer in the 1920s, for example, included these verses in her repertory:

> Columbus discovered America in 1492,
> Then came the English and the Dutch, the Frenchman and
> the Jew.
> Then came the Swede and the Irishman, to help the coun-
> try grow.
> Still they keep on coming, and now everywhere you go—
>
> There's the Argentines and the Portuguese, the Armenians,
> and the Greeks.
> One sells you papers, one shines your shoes,
> Another shaves the whiskers off your cheeks.
> When you ride in the subway train,
> Notice who has all the seats,
> And you'll find they are taken by the Argentine, and the
> Portuguese, and the Greeks.[2]

The native-born looked at immigrant housing—seething with shabby aliens—and grimaced. "Look at how they live!" They saw foreign-language signs on the shops and demanded, "Why don't they learn English?" Nativists contemplated the burgeoning population with hostility and fear and cried, "Those damn foreigners are taking over!"

In one sense, the native-born were correct. Wave after wave of immigrants did "take over" the Lower East Side of New York City, the neighborhood where Bella Spewack began her American journey.

Close to the docks, its first residents were Africans, whose ancestors were the descendants of slaves captured by the Dutch from Portuguese sailing vessels. Germans followed; then Irish. Cantonese men established a community near City Hall. Then Jews and Italians supplanted the Irish and surrounded the Chinese. Today, the majority population continues to be new-comers, now Hispanic and Asian. And once again the native-born, including all too many whose parents or grandparents were themselves immigrants, fear the influx and cry, "Why don't they learn English? Look at how they live!"

How they live? Not well even now. But until public housing began to be constructed in the 1930s, the most likely living quarters for immigrants were in tenements, horrific five- and six-story dwellings that, until laws were slowly passed and owners even more slowly complied, lacked toilets, running water, fire escapes, and landlord-supplied heat and cooking stoves.

The original, pre-law tenements, first erected during the Civil War, also skimped on air and light: only one room in each apartment had windows.

Living conditions could have been worse. The immigrants could have lived on the streets, as our homeless do today. Save for that, and for those fated to live in dank basements, worse housing is hard to imagine. The Golden Land was crosshatched by streets swarming with people, horse-droppings, and push-carts. The sun itself was shrouded by tenements, two deep and side against side.

By 1903, when Fanny Cohen and her daughter Bella arrived in the United States, the tenements had been improved. Now each apartment had, in addition to its windowed "front room"— so called whether it faced the street or the rear of the building— another room that opened onto an air shaft, and interior windows were cut into the walls in order to permit a flow of air. Little by little, the apartments were fitted with piping for illuminating gas. And instead of backyard privies, families got to share indoor toilets, two per four-apartment floor. The law also required that fire escapes be affixed to all the buildings.

America's worst housing? Some scholars, judging from statistics on density and disease, insist it was. Others, thinking of the sod huts inhabited by immigrants in Willa Cather's Nebraska or the shacks of stockyard Chicago and the rural south, say no. What is beyond debate, however, is that these tenements, which housed between twenty and twenty-four families and, all too often, their boarders—usually single men who, in return for a bed, helped pay the rent—were built on twenty-five by one hundred-foot lots originally laid out for single-family homes. And unlike huts and hovels, tenements made a tidy profit for their owners.

Yet for those who didn't die of cholera or from tuberculosis strengthened in its virulence by population density, fetid air, and poor nutrition, living in a tenement on the Lower East Side was not totally dreadful. If opportunities exist that allow for escape, housing in itself can be viewed as a temporary misery.

For Bella, as for generations of immigrants before and since, the escape hatch was education—both what she found for herself and what she was given.

The schools she attended were both ideal and wretched— wretched in their overcrowding (class size was forty-five to fifty); ideal, at least for youngsters like herself, in that they were rigid in their demand that the students seriously attend to learning English.

Although it would be hard to claim that the philosophy of education or methods of teaching were effective for every child among the majority—the 70 percent who were either immigrants or the children of immigrants hailing mostly from Eastern Europe and Italy—the citywide curriculum adopted in 1903 was certainly intended to be beneficial. Even though the school board and other proponents of assimilation were largely motivated by fear and dislike of foreigners, they could still honestly claim that a child's greatest opportunities for success in the United States would come from adopting the new country's culture.

How best could that be done? As quickly as possible. Insist the children learn English, through both the teaching of grammar and vocabulary and the reading of "good" literature. (A decent prose version of Homer's Odyssey was sometimes supplied in the fourth grade, but "good" essentially referred to the works of British writers: Shakespeare, Dickens, Scott, Thackeray, the Brontës, Eliot, Hardy.) English by every and all means.

Simultaneously, instruct them in U.S. and British history so that they can be introduced to "our heritage of institutions and as a reservoir of moral worth." Require the singing of "high class music, as an elevating and inspiring influence." Inculcate "self-reliance and unselfish cooperation" through physical training and athletics.

And see to it that flowing through every subject—from reading and geography to penmanship and civics—run what the school board accepted as commonly held moral and ethical values, values assumed to be lacking in their Yiddish- and Italian-speaking charges. As an associate superintendent of schools put it:

> The school, as one of the instruments of civilization, must take its part in solving the problem that has been precipitated by the great immigration of people who differ from the great mass of our population, not only in language, but in customs, political ideals, and to a considerable extent in religion.[3]

In a further attempt to salvage the little Jews and Roman Catholics, the schools of New York City assumed a progressive slant. They now determined to take the "whole child" and her/his development as their province, although such reform was, of course, slow to filter down to individual schools, principals, and teachers. At least through World War II, most public school children in New York City continued unprogressively to do little more than memorize, pass tests, and behave. Wiggling and slumping were chastised, whispering was reproved, failure to perform correctly often enough meant being "left back." No idle threat on the Lower East Side. Indeed, according to a survey taken in 1904, a year after Bella and her mother arrived in the United States, 38 percent of the city's schoolchildren were overage for their grade. (Not all of this figure can be attributed to nonpromotion; grade placement had frequently to do with capacity to understand the new language. As a result, many twelve-year-olds, humiliated by being taught in the same class as six-year-olds, swiftly dropped out and never returned.)

Another long-lasting feature of this "progressive" education was the inculcation of obedience. Beyond learning to sit quietly with hands folded on their desks, which were bolted to the floor, the young immigrants were put through disciplinary rigors that seem positively prisonlike today.

The routines began when they arrived at school each morning. No horsing around. They were required to line up in order of height on sex-segregated lines and, at the bell, were marched silently to their classrooms. There they hung up their outer garments, sat for the taking of attendance and then, lined up as before, were marched to the assembly hall.

Thomas Hunter, the humane and progressive founding president of the college that now bears his name, thought assembly "the most important single factor in any public institution of learning." As he wrote:

> Here only does the school as a unit come before the principal to receive his orders, to hear his counsel and advice, to listen to a few verses from the Bible (King James version), to sing a non-sectarian hymn and a patriotic song, to imbibe unconsciously a love of English. . . . This assembling is the right beginning of the day with "Order which is heaven's first law."[4]

The children were not only being taught to be Americans, they were being imbued with Protestant values.

Once overwhelmed by immigrants, the schools also took on some responsibility for their health. Hygiene was taught. In addition, heads were examined for nits, eyes were tested for vision, and teeth, though rarely inspected, were supposed to be cared for. The fact of the matter is that many poor children—fearful of adding burdens to the family budget—memorized the eye chart and year after year forged notes from home attesting they had visited the dentist. Only the checking for nits could not be evaded; the cure was an inexpensive application of kerosene or a preparation called "green soap." When the next term, and the next inspection, came, the cure was repeated.

Behave, learn, make a stab at being neat and clean, and *become an American.* Bella bought the package. So did many children. Parents too. Fanny was far from alone in wanting her daughter to become a "lady." Whatever that meant to her, it involved education, specifically in the public schools. Unlike Irish parents, who preferred their children exposed to the various disciplines of parochial schooling; unlike Italian parents, who feared their children might, with education, come to disrespect their elders, Jewish parents held public schooling to be of inestimable value. All education was good, but public school education was best. It was free, it was accessible, it taught the Protestant lifeways of the United States.

Sadly enough, by insisting that their children imbibe the ways of their new country, parents lost authority. We see it in Bella's memoir as she, not her mother, becomes the strength of the household. True, Bella is far more level-headed than Fanny, but her ability to cope with their difficulties can also be attributed to her schooling. It gave her knowledge of American ways. Parents become dependents; children become parents.

When school and home are compatible and consistent, the task of parents in directing, instructing, and shaping their children's lives is relatively easy. When they are not—as they were not in the case of Bella and hundreds of thousands of others—the young abandon what, with the encouragement of schools and settlement houses, they come to view as crude and restrictive "old country" ways. Parents who remain fixed in those ways become less and less relevant. Affection, if it exists, remains while authority dwindles.

Thus the making of Americans.

It is easy, today, to romanticize the time and place. Shuffle together images of Leon Trotsky sipping tea at a workers' cafeteria while Emma Goldman and her lover plot revolution in an upstairs bedroom. Include a fully orchestrated "Alexander's Ragtime Band" (Irving Berlin also hailed from the Lower East Side). Add a street scene: shawled women fingering through goods tumbled on a pushcart; ragged children playing underfoot; a newsboy shouting headlines, ideally something dramatic like "Lusitania Sinks—128 Drown." Add a white-bearded man praying in a synagogue. Add flapping clotheslines. Add a rat scurrying down an alley. . . .

In themselves, the images are authentic, but as Bella Spewack's memoir demonstrates, the facts they represented for her were not up for redemption. The facts added up to a single word: escape.

Most girls escaped, if they did, through marriage. With luck, they would replicate their mothers' lives on a slightly higher income in a better neighborhood. With the extension of rapid transit, often the location of the first move would be Harlem, which in those years was home largely to Jews and Italians. The almost rural neighborhoods of the Bronx and the tree-shaded streets of Brooklyn were also favored. Wherever they went, they'd see to it that their children completed high school with good grades. Only so could they be admitted to New York's two blessedly free colleges—City for boys, the Normal (to be renamed Hunter) for girls—whose aim, like their own, was to educate future doctors and lawyers, accountants and teachers.

Yet remarkably, for those girls who didn't marry immediately out of school, escape was also possible. Some education, much ambition, a lot of luck—again, never forget luck—and off they went to claim their job, their pay envelope, and their future as single women in an environment wider but no less fierce than the Lower East Side.

Did they have dreams beyond the personal? For some, the goal was a just economy—socialism and, in the meanwhile, vigorous labor unions. Others invested their energies in Zionism, in a national home for the Jewish people. Relatively few thought of woman's suffrage as crucially important. The ballot box, despite union engagement, was primarily a middle-class issue. And these immigrant women were not yet middle-class, in many cases not yet citizens. More important than the vote were jobs, pay envelopes, decent working conditions, a future. Families, and younger brothers destined for more education than they themselves were often permitted, relied upon them.

Out of school—they could leave at the age of fourteen or the completion of the sixth grade—girls went into the garment industry and shops. They could aspire to become stenographers, office workers, and department store clerks. With more education, they could try for teaching jobs, to be held until marriage disqualified them, or nursing; or perhaps social work, although that too was thought to be an occupation for the middle class.

Most became what they could imagine becoming. But some among them chose a more dangerous course. They went for broke.

We cannot know what combination of psychic strength and daring allows anyone to project herself into the unknown. Talent, ambition, daring—all are mysteries. But in pondering Bella Spewack's trajectory, we might consider whether father-lessness and tragedy were not in an odd way actual advantages.

To begin with, nature abhors a vacuum. The authority that a father might have wielded, or that a mother less feckless than Fanny should have taken, became Bella's by default. (Was it her "fatherly" example that led her younger brother to become a writer too?) Equally important, did the need, at an early age, to be mature and responsible within the family lead to an inner assumption about her ability to deal with the larger world? It seems reasonable. Further, lacking a father, Bella had no heavy-handed male in her life to announce what she should do or what she must *not* do.

Finally, because the person she cherished most deeply, her brother Herschey, had died, it is likely that she could imagine no pain greater than that which she had already experienced. She had nothing to lose; everything to gain.

Bella, the avid reader, chose to be a writer. Journalism, her first outlet, was neither safe nor steady, but it was a brilliant choice for a word-intoxicated young woman intent on a career. As she must have known, even fame was possible to her there. She had only to think of Nellie Bly, a pioneer among investigative reporters, and of Ida Tarbell, scourge of Standard Oil. What did they have that she didn't?

Except that they were female, everything. They had roots in America. Bella was a poor immigrant Jew at a time when nativism and anti-Semitism were attitudinal standards.

Unless she had launched herself into the garment industry, where Jews were major players, or into the Yiddish theater, then enjoying its greatest American acclaim, or into the strongly masculine domain of labor unions, there was objectively little scope for Bella's ambitions. No old boys' network was in place for the likes of her. No inherited wealth would drop into her cupped hands. No family-bred knowledge of the ways of a profession would illuminate her path.

But lacking such advantages is unlikely to have deterred someone with her "desperado drive." That, supported by implacable schooling and a community in which sources of knowledge were limited to family, friends, and the public library, made selfhood more distinct and hardy than it can be today when film, mass media, wall-to-wall advertising, and cookie-cutter consumerism demand of a youngster that she be and think and dress like others, even in her rebellion.

In that context, Bella probably also benefited from her lack of mentors and "role models." If she did aspire to emulate anyone it would have been journalists like Nellie Bly and Ida Tarbell, or writers like Charlotte Brontë, Louisa May Alcott, and George Eliot, novelists whose work she undoubtedly consumed with the passion of an immigrant child seeking to understand the Anglo-Saxon world. But such women were bred from worlds vastly different from her own. What indeed could Nellie

Bly, the thirteenth child of an Irish-born judge, or the daughter of Bronson Alcott, or a child of the Haworth rectory share with this Hungarian-born ragamuffin roaming the streets of New York? Only their ambition could be accessible to imitation.

Unlike the contemporary youngster gazing starry-eyed at a television image of a "personality" marketed as a role model, Bella could not have cast herself in the image of favorite authors. She could not have duplicated, say, Alcott's hairstyle or Eliot's speech mannerisms or Brontë's shoes. If such were her exemplars, then her choices would have provided inspiration while they allowed her freedom to invent herself.

It is surely odd to consider that multiple poverties—lack of decent housing, of intact family structure, of living exemplars, of money, of higher education, of confident religious belief—might provide energizing psychic freedom. Yet that would seem to be the case here. With no more than a belief in her own talent, supported by a high school education and a library card, Bella dared to go naked into the alien world.

That she succeeded does not, of course, imply that psychic freedom and talent are all that is needed to make one's way in life. Bella also had rare good luck. *The Call* did hire her. (At about the same time, it also hired Dorothy Day, the sainted radical who founded the Catholic Worker movement.) Magazines did publish her fiction. And she soon met and married another writer, a man of character and talent with whom she could collaborate.

While Bella's world is long gone, desperado drive can still catapult an immigrant into success. But although more and better social services are available, the difficulties an immigrant child encounters growing up in New York City today are in many ways significantly greater than those Bella had to face.

As the child of a single parent mired in poverty and ignorance of the larger world, Bella had to cope with that and with her responsibilities for both her mother and brothers. But she did not face what the contemporary immigrant youngster must:

street crime, drugs, a failed educational system combined with a demand by employers for college degrees, a shrunken job market, commercial, other-directed sources of entertainment, and a consumer culture that totally rejects delayed gratification. These contemporary burdens make escape appallingly difficult.

Would Bella have escaped nonetheless? It is nice to think so.

NOTES

1. Eva Hoffman, *Lost in Translation: A Life in a New Language* (New York: E. P. Dutton, 1989).

2. As quoted in Mark Slobin, *Tenement Songs* (Champaign, IL: University of Illinois Press, 1982), 54.

3. From principles set forth by William Maxwell, first superintendent of schools of the consolidated New York City (1898), as a guide to the 1903 curriculum. As quoted in "Schools and the Making of Americans," *Tenement Times* (Summer 1991): 1.

4. *The Autobiography of Thomas Hunter* (New York: The Knickerbocker Press, 1931), 374.

Chronology

1899(?)	Bella Cohen is born in Transylvania on 25 March to Fanny Cohen.
1902(3?)	Bella arrives in New York City with her mother. Their first home is on Cannon Street on the Lower East Side.
1903	Bella makes her theater debut, singing in Victoria Music Hall.
1910	Bella publishes her first article, in the *Courier of P.S. 147*
1911	Fanny marries Noosan Lang.
1912	Bella's half-brother Herschey is born.
1913	Bella's half-brother Daniel is born on Memorial Day.

1917	Bella graduates from Washington Irving High School. She begins her career as a reporter at *Yorkville Home News.*
	Herschey dies.
1918–22	Bella works as a publicity agent and a reporter for several newspapers including *The Call.*
1922	Bella marries Sam Spewack on 17 March.
1922–26	Bella and Sam work as foreign correspondents in Europe. Bella writes her memoir, *Streets,* in 1922 while in Berlin.
1923	Bella returns to New York temporarily and writes a series on slum housing for the *Evening World,* which encouraged the passing of the Rent Laws in New York State.
1925	Bella's story "The Laugh" is selected by Edward J. O'Brien and published in *Best Short Stories of 1925.*
1926	Bella scoops the world with her story on Anna Anderson, who professed to be the last remaining member of the Romanovs, Russia's royal family. The article is published in the *New York Times* and makes headlines around the world.
1927	*The Solitaire Man,* the first play co-written by Bella and Sam, is performed in Boston.
1932	*Clear All Wires!* opens at Times Square

Theater in New York, establishing the Spewacks' career as comedy writers.

1935–36   *Boy Meets Girl* (book by Bella and Sam) opens in New York on 27 November and runs for 669 performances.

1938   *Leave It to Me!* (book by Bella and Sam) with music and lyrics by Cole Porter, opens in New York; in the cast are Mary Martin and Gene Kelly.

Bella helps found the New York Girls' Scholarship Fund.

1940   The film *My Favorite Wife* (story and screenplay by Bella and Sam) featuring Cary Grant is produced by RKO.

1945   The MGM film *Weekend at the Waldorf* (screenplay by Bella and Sam) starring Ginger Rogers and Lana Turner is a box office hit.

1946   As a representative for the United Nations and a reporter for ABC, Bella covers the distribution of food by the United Nations Relief and Rehabilitation Agency in Eastern Europe.

1948   *Kiss Me, Kate* (book by Bella and Sam) with music by Cole Porter opens at the New Century Theater in New York on 30 December.

1949   *Kiss Me, Kate* wins a Tony Award, the first given to a musical. It goes on to become a national and international success, performed in translation in over twenty-two countries.

1953   *Kiss Me, Kate* is made into an MGM film.

My Three Angels (book by Bella and Sam), a comedy adapted from Albert Husson's play *La Cuisine des Anges,* opens on 11 March at the Morosco Theater in New York. It runs for 344 performances and is later produced in London, Israel, and Mexico.

1960   Bella and Sam found the Spewack Sports Club for the Handicapped in Ramat Gan, Israel.

1971   Sam Spewack dies in New York City.

1990   Bella Cohen Spewack dies in New York City.

Compiled in part from the catalog for the exhibition *From Russia to "Kiss Me Kate": The Careers of Sam and Bella Spewack* (New York: Columbia University Office of Publications, 1993).

Broome Street, Elizabeth to Berry, 1920. (United States History, Local History & Geneology Division, The New York Public Library, Astor, Lenox, and Tilden Foundations)

Bella in the country, 1916.

Top right: Bella's half-brother, Herschey Lang, age 5, the year of his death (1917).

Top left: Bella's half-brother, Daniel Lang, circa 1928.

Left: Bella's mother, Fanny (Cohen) Lang, circa 1940.

Bella and Sam, Berlin, 1923.

*Orchard Street,
circa 1914.*

Left: Sam Spewack, 1924.

Bottom: Rivington Street, Columbia to Cannon, 1920.

(United States History, Local History & Geneology Division, The New York Public Library, Astor, Lenox, and Tilden Foundations)

Bella and Sam, 1969; their last picture together.
(Cookie Snyder, Winston-Salem, NC)

Bella, 1975.

Except where noted: all photos courtesy of the Samuel and Bella Spewack Papers, Rare Book and Manuscript Library, Columbia University; by permission of Arthur and Lois Elias.

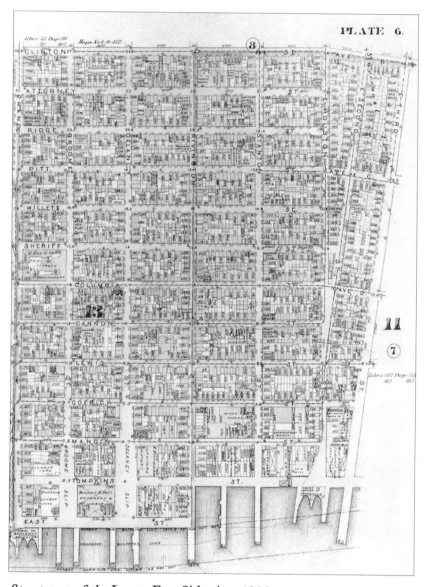

Street map of the Lower East Side, circa 1900.

(Courtesy of Avery Architectural and Fine Arts Library, Columbia University in the City of New York)

Streets

Prologue

I feel pains," my mother said to my father. They were both at a ball and the music rang in my mother's ears, for she had been dancing too much.

"Very well then, Fanny, we'll go home," my father said with a sigh. He did not like to leave the ball before the evening was half over.

I was born half an hour later.

When my mother knew I was here, she reached out for the delicately sharpened pencils she had kept on the little table near the bed ever since she knew I was coming.

"What are you going to do?" the nurse and doctor exclaimed in surprise.

"I am going to make her dimples," my mother said. She was only seventeen.

"But she already has them," the doctor said gravely, and my mother thanked him and went to sleep.

They were living in a little house in a town near Bucharest.

Two weeks later, my father skipped off with our servant, who was twenty years his senior.

A rabbi divorced my mother from my father, "since God so willed." Then my mother bought me a red dress and got passage on a ship for America called Fiume.

PART I

Cannon Street

Cannon Street was the first of the streets on the Lower East Side that life scooped out for me. It stretches out of Grand Street north past Broome, Delancey, Rivington, and Stanton into Houston—a narrow gutter, flanked by narrower sidewalks. On the other side of Grand Street, where I used to go Saturday nights to buy my hair ribbons, it ascends like a runway in a theater. At the corner rose the sugary odors of a pie factory.

On the other side of Houston Street, a street of noble width, Cannon Street narrows and narrows until it is but the wink of a blind man's eye: Manhattan Street.*

Thousands of people live on Cannon Street, occupying rear houses and front houses from basement to top floor. The houses are sour with the smell of crowded human flesh. So many words were spoken that words meant little. Blows meant more.

On this street, I spent the first ten years of my life.

On this street, I learned to fear people.

---

*Neither Cannon nor Manhattan Street exists any longer. Cannon disappeared when the Amalgamated Clothing Workers sponsored livable housing in the 1930s. Manhattan Street most likely is covered by the Lillian Wald Houses. —R.L.

We landed in New York and were greeted by a short, frail blond man with pink-threaded cheeks. He told me that he was my cousin but he was not. My mother and I spent the first night in a bed with two others in a room back of the restaurant kept by Channeh Rosenthal. Her little girl was a waxen, famished-looking creature who was always whining for her "mommeh" and sucked her thin thumb. She was older than I was by two years. I remember her sulking jealousy of my red dress.

I could sing well in Hungarian and German and spoke a broken Romanian as well as a smooth, declamatory Yiddish. Before long I could mutter realistically English oaths. For all these, the patrons of Channeh Rosenthal's restaurant would pay me in coppers which I dutifully handed over to my mother.

My mother did not stay long in Channeh Rosenthal's restaurant. She went to an employment agency on Fourth Street between Avenues C and B, one of a number on the block. The same string of employment offices exists today with their blatant blue and white painted signs—"SERVANTS"— jutting out from the top level of the stores in which they are located.

I grew restive under the enforced waiting of three monotonous days. Mother and I would arrive in the morning, wait until twelve when we would go out and buy an apple from a street peddler, return and wait until four, and finally return home. I would play outside by myself or accept overtures from the "Yankee" children after they had teased me to their hearts' content.

When I grew tired I would sit on the floor of the office and watch. Employers, usually the womenfolk, would come down to interview applicants. Did the girl like children? Could she cook? Frequently the ever-ready assistant would be dispatched for a fortunate girl's suitcase left with her landlady. Sometimes the latter would refuse to give up the suitcase and would herself come down to the office. The girl owed her money. Who would pay her? Oh, the girl had a job! Well, the valise could go, but not before the address of the girl's situation is written out "black on white." Meanwhile the girl would be glancing apologetically at the face of her prospective employer and pluck at her hands in fear.

Then the employer, the newly hired servant, and the assistant with the suitcase would be off together in an uneven line.

We had to wait and wait because no one wanted a servant with a child.

Finally our turn came.

We went to the house of a man who wore his tightly curled hair parted in the middle. When he smiled, he kept his pink lips shut and wrinkles chased themselves across his face like ripples on water. His wife was in the hospital and Mother was to be the servant until his wife returned and was well enough to take care of the house and the three children.

I don't remember seeing any children, but I do remember the peculiar arresting odor of leather in the house. Of the day we spent there, I know nothing. At night, I remember my mother complained of the weariness she felt after scrubbing those five rooms and feeding the children. But we were glad to have found a temporary haven. Then she and I went to sleep.

Perhaps two hours later, I was awakened by the voice of my mother, shrill and sharp with indignation. By the side of the bed, stood her employer. . . .

We finished the rest of the night in the bed of Channeh Rosenthal, after my mother had wept her story and received Channeh's pitying cluckings.

Again, we went to the employment office and waited for work.

By this time, it was summer and my mother went to work in the house of a middle-aged, sharp-eyed couple in Canarsie for sixteen dollars. These people kept a counter and restaurant, serving seafood, frankfurters, popcorn, etc. They had three sons, two of whom helped in the business, and the third, who was in the throes of a disease that makes people grow too much (I don't know what it is called), did nothing but sit on the beach and throw sand into the water after he had carefully molded it into a ball. There was an adopted daughter besides, a tall soft-breasted girl of seventeen who had hair the color of prune soup. She giggled when the diners talked to her and parted the wave in her pompadour with a pink, long-fingered hand.

I wandered about at my own will becoming a familiar and welcome figure in the beer gardens that at the time were as much a part of Canarsie as the salty air. In these beer gardens, one could order a mug and see a vaudeville show on the strength of one order. I would run errands for some of the actors and actresses and be paid liberally. I would imitate them and they would throw back their heads and laugh and I was happy. Very happy. I liked to make people laugh.

It was close to the end of the summer when something happened to hasten our departure. Mother and I shared the bed with Celia, the adopted daughter of our employers. Throughout our stay, there had always been bedbugs, but on that night, they seemed to have called a mass meeting, as Celia observed with her giggle.

I fell asleep while my mother mounted watch over me. It was in one of those half-veiled snatches of sleep that I felt the need of my mother's protecting hand on my uncovered feet. I opened my eyes and saw Celia sitting up against the wall, her arms crossed over her bosom, her hair falling about her like moon mist. She wore no nightgown but a short, thin petticoat and her shirt. My mother was moving about on the floor feeling her way to the matches. I could see everything by the white light that came from the night sky.

"I can't find them," my mother cried. "Where are the matches? I can't find the matches."

"You want the matches?"

My body stiffened. That was a new voice . . . a man's voice.

"She wants the matches!" said a second new voice . . . a man's voice. It was mocking and ugly.

"Let 'er look," added a third new voice. It belonged to the boy who was growing to death.

And suddenly through the dark room sped lighted matches deftly flipped from the corners of the room. I screamed as one touched me. Celia was crying and laughing wildly, while my mother shrieked and shouted, "If I only had a knife, I would stick it into you, murderers! God should punish you for what you are doing to a poor orphan." The orphan was Celia.

I do not remember how the night ended, and I will not ask my mother. She would probably lie about it and perhaps try to laugh—not to reassure me, but herself.

Three days later, we left. Celia wept when my mother left but shook her head when Mother asked her to go away with us.

"Where could I go? This is the only home I know. Oh, don't worry about me. I don't belong to anyone. No one cares what happens to me."

Then she began to giggle and patted the wave in her pompadour.

When we returned, we stayed with a woman whom my mother called the Peckacha, in a rear house on Ridge Street. She was a pock-marked, toothless woman of thirty-two who was always pressing her bladderlike breast to the mouth of a reluctant, sallow baby. Her husband had the saintly, shadowy look of a prophet. His face was delicately gaunt, with two deep-set, pale blue eyes and blond whiskers that grew at random, like grass in rocky ground. He was a baker. He slept during the day so Mother and I were able to sleep in his bed at night.

There were many children who, from the oldest—a long-legged and freckled-faced girl—to the two-year-old Mechel, who would wander out into the street as he was created, did nothing but swear at each other. They all had great dark slimy eyes as if gutter mud had been slapped into their faces and broad noses.

They pinched me and slapped me just as they did one

another. Only when I "acted" for them did they give me peace.

The figure of a slight, sallow girl whose black dress merges into the shadows of my memory will not evade me. She lived underneath us, boarding with an old man and his wife. I cannot remember this girl ever smiling—not even her eyes. They were like still, stagnant sewer pools in her V-shaped yellow face. Her hair she wore like the girls of the day, in a pompadour to the front and a Psyche knot in the back. She always seemed to be resting her slight weight against the side of the open door—never going out into the street, frequently retreating with frightened backsteps into the yard. I never saw her during the daytime.

My mother called her "the night birdie."

My mother did not like me to go with her to the employment offices and so she left me behind to the mercies of the young Peckachas. I avoided them as much as possible. I was afraid of them.

I found living on the floor below us a fat man with a wooden leg who could play the accordion melodiously well. He played Romanian folk music mostly but now and then would change the programme to include "Take a Car," then in vogue. The Peckacha children dubbed him my "fella." When I did not seem to mind, they stopped calling him that, and after they discovered that I was honorable—I did not betray them when they lied or when they beat a child younger than themselves—they took me with them on one of their forages to Attorney Street. Attorney Street, like Orchard Street, is a market where fruit and vegetable dealers sell to the street and store vendors. Cases, bulging with oranges or apples and watermelon, line the streets, while men with live, dirty hands darted among them with eyes that took in everything. People live on these streets as well, rotting in their cases with the overripe fruits.

The Peckacha children went in a group. Manny, the oldest boy, pointed out a case of large ripe oranges to me.

"You see that place where the stick is broke? Go over there

an' take an orange," said Manny. "If you get it, run." His nose resembled a round mass of putty, wet and gray. He drew it up in the manner of one who knows that he was talking to a faint heart. Then they all walked to the corner and waited for me.

I walked to the case and without even looking around, stuck my hand into the aperture and plucked a large, overripe orange. My heart pounded against me. I wanted to run, but my feet were stuck to the ground. There I stood with the stolen orange in my hand.

"Go to hell, run!" shouted Manny.

I threw the orange at him and ran in the opposite direction.

My mother found a new situation at fourteen dollars a month in a home where there were two little girls of my own age. I remember nothing of this home, except its cleanliness and that the "boss" was a jovial, middle-sized fellow who always brought me what he brought his two little girls. When my mother took the children and me for a walk after her work in the kitchen was over, we always stopped outside a large fruit and grocery store. The memory of its clean, spicy smell still stays with me. Above us, at intervals rumbled the "L."

Then Mother decided that she wanted to work in a shop . . . that cooking, housework, and washing were a little too much for her. The middle-sized man was not jovial now but long-faced and offered to give her a raise if she would only stay.

But my mother had made up her mind to go. She was really meant to be a rover, and the idea of going to work in a factory had taken possession of her. Although I did not understand everything she told me, I comprehended some of her arguments. First, in a shop, she would have so many hours to work and then she would go home and be her own boss. Second—repeat the first argument; third, repeat the second argument and add, one could see friends besides.

She found work as an operator in a ladies' shirtwaist shop at $7.50 a week.

I was afraid that I would have to go back to the Peckacha children, but Mother had found a Mrs. Pincus, a widow on Cannon Street near Delancey Street, who possessed an only, hulking, tongue-tied daughter, Clara. Mrs. Pincus was a pious old lady who possessed large glass earrings that bore a striking resemblance to her eyes. She wore a wig with a ribbon atop it, or perhaps it was just a black lace covering worn green with constant use. Her eyes were sore and always filled with water, lending a certain suitable trimming to her show of dreary piety.

Her daughter, Clara, also had sore eyes, but hers seemed to be in a constant state of shriveling up. Her lids were always red with the lashes sticking together in straight, upward strokes. Clara went to school, and although she went unwillingly, I laid at her feet my worship for her scholastic prowess. I longed for the day when I would be able to go to school.

My mother and I were given the bed that, during the day, was a bureau burdened down by glass pitchers and painted glasses, making up lemonade and punch sets. In the morning, my mother would wake me up crying that she had to do so.

"You look so pretty in your sleep. It breaks my heart to make your eyes open. You look at me with such reproach," my mother would sigh. She would press warm milk to my sleepy lips and then dress me hurriedly, but not carelessly. Then, because I was barely able to stand upon my numb feet, my mother would half drag, half carry me to the Brightside Day Nursery on the next block.

The first day I was introduced there, Miss Rachel, the matron, a broad-hipped, small-faced woman, patted my head and assured my mother that her baby would be well taken care of.

"Haben sie keine Furcht?" she asked in a soft, gutteral German.

My mother bent reverently at that and kissed her plump hand.

There were many other children like me, whose mothers worked during the day. Them, their husbands had deserted.

Others were widows with memories of love words and deathbeds.

The nursery building, of gray stone, imperturbably restful, clean, and calm-eyed, stands out on Cannon Street to this day, a thing apart from its neighbors.

We children were herded into the basement by our parents, who left us there. It was gloomy but much warmer than the rooms all of us had just left. Our mothers and some fathers would risk being late and docked for a few moments to breathe in the luxuriant warmth that came from the walls.

Mothers who had infants would go upstairs to the nursery with the sleeping babes in their arms. I can imagine how they felt when the children, slipping from their caressing grasp, uttered low cries, opened startled eyes, and reassured, fell back into their clean cribs into sleep again. Sometimes, the babies cried long, unrelenting wails and mothers would steal through our midst in the basement, their hands to their eyes.

Then Miss Fannie came down. She had long red cheeks, and black, laughing eyes with chimney-black frowsy hair that stood out about her head. Her striped blue dress with its white apron was to me the embodiment of all splendor. I later mentally fitted all my princesses with Miss Fannie's uniform.

Upstairs we went to don our checked pinafores that covered us from chin to knee, and some to shoe tops. Then we sang "Father, We Thank Thee."

The room here was large and yellow-floored with a stained window in the rear corner through which the sun never shone. Gay paper chains decorated the walls. There was also a piano, a mysterious thing that cried and laughed when Miss Fannie touched it. (I had surely seen a piano in Canarsie but it had made no impression, probably outclassed by the brass instruments and the drum.) Behind this room, across a hiccough of a hall, was the dining room where long low tables and green-painted "baby" chairs were lined.

Here at noon we seated ourselves, folded our hands over the table, and bent our heads over our hands. Under the prompting guidance of Miss Fannie or Miss Rachel, we thanked God for many things, none of which I remember, at least not indelibly. We always had hot watery cocoa, prunes, and rice served in gray tin dishes.

I don't know how many children and babies the Brightside Day Nursery held, but they were many—too many for me to remember. So that today, I have only the memory of a pallid, gray-eyed little girl of my own age and a red-headed boy of six who would get under the table and pinch our legs. The girl always screamed but would never tell the reason to Miss Fannie. When the boy pinched my legs, I kicked him.

At night, from six to seven, we would file down to the basement where our clothing hung and try to play. Each time the door opened we would lift our eyes, leaping with fondness. Then, as it turned out not to be our particular mother or father, we would turn back to our sitting games and wait for the next gust of wind.

Most of the younger ones' mothers would try to drop a curtsey. My mother always tried to kiss the hand of Miss Rachel or Miss Fannie. The older ones, a little harder than the rest, would take their children by the hand and throw their snapped goodnights over their shoulders.

When it snowed, I would always slide my way home, while my mother would run after me, crying: "Bella, Bella, you'll fall down and break a leg!"

After the first week in Mrs. Pincus's basement, my mother arranged to have Mrs. Pincus wake me and give me hot milk while she herself hurried off to the shop.

From the first day that this duty fell upon her, the old lady took a particular delight in pulling my ears to make me open my eyes. But I clung to sleep and closed my eyes again. With a stifled indignant cry that set the bow on her wig all atremble, she pulled the covers from me and dragged me to the floor, kneading her fingers into my arms and back. By this time I was awake and aching.

Her daughter, Clara, was asleep in the next room. I could hear her rasping snore as I dressed with chilled fingers. At that moment, I envied stupid Clara, lying with her hand over her nose and her eyelids partially drawn over her eyes. At the end of the second week, Mrs. Pincus began taking my ribbons from me with the order that I keep my mouth shut.

I did not tell my mother. She had her own troubles. Her mother was imploring her in bi-monthly letters to send more money. A younger sister was to be married. The dowry had to be provided. Besides, I was afraid that we would have to move back to those Peckacha children.

I felt instinctively Mrs. Pincus's blows were preferable to their slimy mouths.

So I watched my ribbons disappear into the secretive-looking bundles that Mrs. Pincus stored under her bed until one night I could stand it no longer. There was a bruise on my back that burned me as if I had been branded by a red-hot iron.

My mother turned me over anxiously and began to cry. She cried easily.

"Honeyle, you are black and blue and your skin is peeled from your bones!" she exclaimed. Just then Mrs. Pincus entered from the rear room. My mother pointed to my uncovered back while her tears fell hot upon it.

"Look, Mrs. Pincus. Look! Would you believe that a kindergarten could do such things?" she cried out. I had not said the kindergarten had inflicted those marks on my body, but my mother had already decided that for herself. Who else but the kindergarten? Burned it should be!

My mother rubbed some salve on my back and turned me over, crooning and moaning. Then she went to sleep. I tried to whisper to her and nudged her but she was exhausted from work and the unexpected sight of my blemished back. I lay awake all night so that I should not miss my mother in the morning, but I fell asleep. When I awoke my mother had already left.

Mrs. Pincus did not attempt to hasten my dressing the usual way although she did not omit the usual tweaking of my ears. She even permitted me to wear the new ribbon my mother had brought me the night before. I drew back suspiciously from an attempted pat. Mrs. Pincus might have changed her mind before her hand rested on my hair.

All day I was unusually silent in the kindergarten. Since I was excused from any of the games that required much exercise, because of my back, I had plenty of time to brood on my decision to tell my mother the truth. When she came that night, she sullenly refused to return the "good evening" that Miss Fannie extended her. Her lips began to tremble. I was afraid she would cry and I did not want Miss Fannie to see my mother cry! So on the pretense of having her help me locate my coat and tam o' shanter, I took her to the wardrobe closet and told her the truth.

She was so stunned that for a moment she could do nothing but stare at me.

"You tell me the truth?" she asked.

"She's got the ribbons too," I added.

This was too much. My mother rushed from me with the tale of my tortures to Miss Fannie and Miss Rachel.

"Now, if you can't trust a religious woman who wears a wig, whom can you trust?" she tearfully demanded.

One of the mothers who had crowded around her told her of a Mrs. Forman who lived in a rear house opposite who would be glad to have us board with her.

My mother immediately went to meet Mrs. Forman, who proved to be a little woman of fifty with curling black bangs over her forehead. She had a long nose and thin little pale lips that she sucked continually. She put her arms around me and asked my mother where she had gotten such a pretty daughter.

My mother left me in her care and went to get our belongings from Mrs. Pincus's basement. In about a half hour she returned, her cheeks streaked with tears and her eyes blazing with stored-up wrath. Two small boys followed her with our featherbed and valises. As she paid them, she burst out into wild curses, invoking all the black years with their pestilences to fall upon the head of the pious, watery-eyed Mrs. Pincus.

Mrs. Forman transferred her pats to my mother's head. With every murmured word of sympathy, she screwed up her funny little grey eyes until they seemed to be just mere scintillating pinpoints of light. Why dwell on unhappy things that are past? Better to forget. . . . God had already punished Mrs. Pincus. Did my mother know that Mrs. Pincus had had an older daughter, who had run away from her to Philadelphia? Yes, with a man. And her mother had never heard from her since.

"Beauty is like a curse," Mrs. Forman said in her little voice. It came as if she were pressing her lips against a knothole in a fence. "If her daughter had not been so beautiful, she would still be at the side of her mother. Now, my daughter no one will ever take from me. She is so ugly."

And Mrs. Forman was truthfully open-eyed. Yetta, her daughter, was a red-haired, long-nosed, slanty-eyed girl with round shoulders and a pitiful desire to be in style. Her eyelashes and brows were the color of her freckles, of which she had a large ill-proportioned number. She later married—or rather was married to—a widower with three children, who wiped his nose on his sleeve.

While we were staying at Mrs. Forman's, Mother began to attend what was known briefly as "dancing." It was not dancing school, or dancing hall, but just "dancing." Her friends, girls whom she had looked down upon in her native town, introduced her to the dancing.

The hall was located on Columbia Street, just one block ahead of ours. Winderlow's was like other dancing schools atop a saloon. Ladies 10¢, Gents 15¢. My mother took me with her and told me to call her auntie. Sometimes when she was surrounded by several men wearing collars much too large for them, I would open my mouth threateningly and shape the word "Momma," and my mother would take my hand in hers and hold it tight.

It would be midnight before we returned. Mother was a graceful little dancer, fond of showing the steps she knew in Europe although she was just as much at home in the "American" waltz.

One night my mother told me to go up into the balcony and wait for her. She would be up directly to get her coat. I waited for a while leaning upon the balcony railing and singling out my mother on the dancing floor. It was the last dance, the one where the women asked the men for the privilege and pleasure of the next dance. As Mother walked across the hall to the men's row of seats, three of them rose as one and surrounded her. Mother deliberately left them and walked over to the seat of a shy, red-faced fellow who had been kneading his fingers awkwardly upon his drawn-up knees.

Then the dance began.

As I did not care to watch the dance, I began to wander around to the more remote precincts of the balcony. Some girls were sitting chattering in the women's dressing room and fixing their faces up for the street. They did not interest me and I wandered on to the far corner of the balcony. It was not lit at all, for no one ever went there. Its darkness attracted me, tired with lack of sleep.

I drew back suddenly when I heard voices . . . a man's and a woman's.

"I tell you to put me down," breathed the woman's. "Put me down. I'm afraid. They will find us here and what will become of me? I tell you to put me down."

"Sh-sh," was all the man said. "Sh-sh."

There was a scuffle and then, "Oh, I know you're stronger than I am. Please, please. Stop! Stop!"

In bed that night, I could not sleep. That woman's voice with its hysterical pleading and the man's thick tones. Why was she afraid?

I began to cry.

My mother turned over, and I could feel her eyes upon me in the dark.

"What's the matter?" she asked me in Yiddish.

"Matter?" I repeated fiercely. "Nothing. Only this. You can go yourself dancing. You leave me in the house. I tell you I won't go. Go yourself."

My mother picked me up in her arms.

"Did anyone touch you?" she whispered shrilly.

At that moment, I despised her.

"No," I replied, disgusted. Why was she always so quick to guess the dirty things?

"Then it's something else."

I told her.

"Honeyle, I will never go again. I swear to God. From tonight on, I'm through," my mother said in such a loud voice that Mrs. Forman came in to see what was wrong. Reassured she went back to sleep, and soon my mother and I followed her example.

In the morning when I opened my eyes, I heard my mother saying to Mrs. Forman, "Such a thing wouldn't have happened had I a home of my own. It's because I have no home of my own that I go to dancing and stay up late and make the eyes of my head old before their time. I thought it out last night, Mrs. Forman. I'll take in a few boarders and I'll sew. That will pay the rent and give me food. No? I can see nothing else better. To roam from house to house as a servant I don't even wish my enemies to enjoy. And in the shop, let those who wish me evil, work. I will take rooms and give her a home. She will soon be going to school and I will have to be home now. It would not be right to have her in the streets after three o'clock. She sees too much."

My mother was afraid of the thing that was striking terror into my own heart—my seeing too much. At the time, I thought that there was something evil in me that attracted evil to it.

On the same block, just two houses nearer Rivington Street, a new building had been erected. My mother took a strong fancy to it. I guess it was the idea that the building in its clean fresh state would help her to start anew. A three-room apartment (bedroom, kitchen, and dining room, with a toilet in the apartment, not in the hall or in the yard such as we had always been accustomed to) was rented, and Mother set up house with the little she had saved.

My mother's boarders, so far as the women were concerned, were transient. They were servant girls, most if not all Hungarians who, having disagreed with their "missus" or deciding to leave having tired of their situations, came to rest at my mother's until they found a new place. They paid ten cents a night to sleep, sharing the bed with another girl in the dining room or sleeping with my mother and myself in the bedroom when we were crowded. In the winter they sometimes slept on the floor and in the summer on the fire escape.

The men boarders all slept in the kitchen on two folding beds. Sometimes there were four, sometimes there were three, but there was always some gross, domineering boarder about. They were recruited from the *landsleit*, mother's friends of the old country, or from a group of stalwart Russian "mercenaries." One of them, Bennie, fat and pink-mouthed, worked in a cloak shop as an operator during the day and at night spent his time in the saloon or helping his numerous friends settle their private feuds. Another one, known as Dimmi, did not work at all, but would mysteriously at certain intervals arrive with a blue-ringed eye and once with a permanently broken nose.

Those were the offensive ones.

The inoffensive ones included a blond-bearded, blue-eyed religious Jew, Yuntl, who, driven by the growth of a wisdom tooth, got drunk for the first and only time and was so ashamed that he stayed away for two weeks. Another, Mucya, thirsting for gold and adventure, had himself shipped to a small town to work on the railroad through one of the Bowery agencies. When he came back, the group in our house was torn between pity and derision for him. For Mucya was very sick and he talked no more of his desire for gold and adventure. It had been driven out of him in that far-off small town.

I remember when the talk would veer to America, as it always did, he would say, "Yes, you think America is here, but I know better. The real America is where I was with niggers and Irishers and Taliayners* sleeping on the floor in one room. That's where the real America is. This is the gilded frame."

Mucya took a certain pride in his sorry adventure, but strangely enough he never would tell of it. It was enough for him that he had suffered.

Among the servant girls who stayed with us was Sadie, brown-skinned, gray-eyed, whose fine teeth were beginning to yellow near the gums. Sadie was in love with an audacious black-haired fellow who mysteriously stopped coming to see her when word was whispered that she had visited him in his bedroom. He had sometimes brought with him a silent, heavy-jawed Litvak who would stare at Sadie with the eyes of a dying fish. This friend began paying court to her in a silent dreary way. Once Sadie took me to the movies and confided to me that she hated him. She married him and I believe they now have many children.

There was little Frieda who never could find her corset and would garb her squat, loosely fat figure in a kimono. Whenever I think of her, I can smell the sweat that tickled her armpits and the line where her hair fringed her forehead. She could sit for hours in her wrapper, after her breakfast, and look out of the window. Our windows faced the back. She could see

---

*Italians —*B.S.*

nothing except clothes lines and laundry handing out to dry. But there she would sit, now and then murmuring, "Where can that corset be?"

Little Frieda was kind to me.

There was Gussie, who had a pert little red nose and a permanent cold. She always wore two little ruffled pads on her flat chest. She was by far the wittiest and the cleanest of those I can remember. Once she brought me a pair of silk gloves that she had stolen from the little daughter of her mistress, and the next time she came, she brought me several pretty ribbons.

"Take them," she said to me with a slight push. "You like us when we give you ribbons, don't you? And when we don't, we can all go to grass. Hah?"

I was holding a book close to me (it told all about the country and a pair of twins who were invited to spend the summer there). I did not attempt to deny what Gussie said. It was true. I despised all of my mother's boarders and clearly indicated it. I was called a snob in various languages and intonations.

"You watch, Fanny," said one of my mother's *landsleit* to her on one occasion when I refused to shake hands with them. "You watch, she will say some day that you are not her mother, mark my words."

One hot night when I could not sleep, I could hear hushed voices and moving beds. My mother opened her eyes when there was a sudden shriek of laughter.

"Stay here," she said to me.

I remained in bed but my mother's voice told me all that my eyes might have seen.

"Do you not feel any shame? Why do you do this? Isn't my life hard enough without your besmirching my name? Put those beds back where they belong and you, Mollie, take your things and don't let me ever see you again. Frieda . . ."—my mother was crying by this time—"I had thought of you as a decent, respectable girl. Shame upon you."

Strangely enough, my mother said nothing to the men. She was afraid of them. They all owed her money for food and lodging, and Dimmi and Bennie could have easily broken in some night and smashed her furniture to pieces.

Of the school days that were a part of these home days, I can only recall the fat, white-faced, fragrant Miss Houston who made me cry. I liked to go to school. I liked the neutral odor of the place; its dim, stone-floored playground; its many round pillars; its cagelike staircases and its stiff, drowsy silences.

My teacher, Miss Beeh, had sent me with a note and an explanation to Miss Houston, another teacher of the 2B grade at the other end of the hall. I had just begun my explanation when Miss Houston stretched out a white arm and motioned me away and to silence.

"Stop," she said aloud so that the whole class heard. "You smell of onions!"

I stopped, and out in the hall I cried softly and argued with myself. What was the matter with onions? Weren't they the same as potatoes or apples or bread?

Didn't she know onions made you feel as full as if you'd eaten meat?"

One day, the Lovely Lady came to the house. She wanted my mother to repair several of her theatrical dresses. Paula was her name. She had clear gray eyes shaped like a pear cut open, white skin, and hair the color of fresh applesauce. Her teeth were white and she smiled often. She aroused all the romance in me because she was so lovely and because she was an actress. She did "single turns" in a vaudeville house on Clinton Street. She taught me how to sing "For Sale, a Baby," and let me finger the dress my mother was fixing for her. It was her stage dress and was brilliant and light with tinsel.

Hers was a murky history and yet she herself was as smooth-skinned and untroubled as a toothless baby. At the age of fifteen she was sold to a peasant by her mother who was burdened by eleven younger children. Two years later she ran away from him to a large city and went to live with the son of a Jewish merchant. He took her to America with him. At the end of a year she was living with two Italians who finally killed each other in a row over her. She was found weeping in the street by one of the circle, Nicker.

Nicker measured six-foot four, boasted often and simply of his strength in the iron foundry in which he worked and of how the mere sound of his voice threw terror into the hearts of his listeners.

"When I say to a man, 'Give me five dollars!'" Nicker would frequently declare, "he will put his hands into his pockets and give me whatever he has there. And sometimes, my friends, there is more than what I ask for."

Despite the fact that he boasted so much, Nicker was really a brave fellow. He never received a blow without giving back three for it.

The Lovely Lady did not love Nicker. She was grateful to him for helping her in her distress, but now that she was earning enough money at the vaudeville theater to save a bit besides, she wanted him to leave her. But Nicker had conceived a jealous love for her. He gave up his job at the foundry and followed her to and from the theater and watched her perform. If he found any man attempting to pay attentions to her, he would take him aside and tell him her story, not troubling to omit even a single detail. If this did not keep the man away, he would dodge him until he got him to a comparatively lonely street where he would beat him.

The man would never come back to watch the Lovely Lady in her turn.

Nicker began to look haggard. His clothes lost their trimness and sagged with the flesh on his cheeks. But the Lovely Lady did not even want to talk to him.

He came to my mother.

Would she talk to the Lovely Lady?

My mother said she wouldn't. "What do you want with her?" she asked indignantly. "Haven't you a wife of your own in Europe?"

In five minutes, Nicker had overcome my mother's objections to pleading his cause by the threat that he would not stop at breaking up everything she had in the flat but that he would extend his arguments to my mother herself. That night my mother went to see Paula in a house on Broome Street. She took me with her. We went up several flights of stairs and knocked at a door.

"It's me, Fanny," my mother said. "Let me in."

A moment later the door was opened. We found the Lovely Lady sitting at ease at a white-covered table just finishing a little lunch after the theater. There was a shining red apple on the table. She did not have to go back until the next day. She sat in a loose, bright-colored wrapper, her hair down her back. She was so very lovely that I could not resist patting her arm as it lay on the table. She caressed me and asked me whether I remembered the song she had taught me.

My mother was trying to appear at ease with the Lovely Lady's aunt. The woman was not an aunt, but the Lovely Lady called her that because she liked to feel she belonged to someone. She was just her landlady.

As she finished her food, Paula turned to my mother with an inquiring smile. "He sent you to talk to me, didn't he?" she asked.

My mother nodded and lowered her eyes. She was probably thinking of the wife in Europe.

The Lovely Lady began to laugh.

"He will kill you if he sees you going with anyone else. So much he loves you," my mother pleaded.

The Lovely Lady trilled her laugh, her last note pitched high.

Oh to be like her! I wished.

Then the door began to tremble, and before we could recover from our surprise, it had been forced open. Nicker stood at the opening, his eyes, red with lack of sleep, fixed upon the Lovely Lady.

"You laugh?" he said to her, and he looked as if he were going to cry.

For an answer she laughed again, her last note pitched even higher.

Then I don't know from where—or how he could have appeared so silently—an immense Negro entered and caught up the Lovely Lady in his arms and went out with her.

"Don't you dare try to get out of this house before I come back," Nicker said. "If you do, there are three men waiting for you on the other side of the street."

They were there as he said.

When Nicker returned, he put some money into the hands of the aunt and simply motioned my mother to follow him from the flat. I stumbled in their rear. It was past midnight.

My mother said nothing. She was too deeply moved to pretend speech.

After a while, Nicker began to talk.

"Did you see the way that nigger picked her up?" He chuckled grimly. "I once did that nigger a favor and he didn't forget to pay back, Fanny. He didn't forget to pay back. He didn't hurt her. He picked her up as if she had been a baby. Just like he was a cradle and she was a baby. If he had hurt her, I would have blown the brains out of his black head."

Nicker began to moan and his large body trembled. "She is so beautiful," he whimpered. "She is so beautiful. She is so beautiful. I would have carried her myself but she has weakened me so."

He stopped uncertainly and dug his fists into his eyes. "My God, how I love her!" he bellowed to the stars.

My mother now began to talk of getting married.

"If I were married, I would not be threatened all the time," she said to Mrs. Taub, her right-hand neighbor. "It is not good for my child to hear that."

Mrs. Taub, who was very fat and freckled, agreed with my mother that she ought to marry and went to the extent of bringing her a suitor, a very rich man from Philadelphia, visiting New York. I remember his coming particularly. He was very small and swarthy and wore a dirty white cotton tie under his frayed collar.

My mother looked very pretty and clean in a new, white lawn shirtwaist she had made for herself. When she saw the gnarled little fellow, she was so disappointed that she could barely force herself to talk to him. Mrs. Taub attempted to create a bridge of conversation, but failed until the prospective suitor ordered the blinds to be drawn.

"But why?" my mother, startled, asked.

"You will see," was the oracular response of the man from Philadelphia. He pulled the blinds down himself and then asked my mother to come close.

"You too," he said to me. Mrs. Taub was as close as her fat body and her married state permitted her to be. Her thin, white-faced husband peeked over her shoulder. My mother stood aloof. The little man took from the bosom of his shirt a grimy handkerchief. He untied that and we saw a dirt-streaked sock that smelled strangely sweet and sour.

"Come here, little girl," he said to me. "Hold up your skirt."

I did so and he poured a thin stream of gold coins into the improvised basin.

His look became ardent as he addressed my mother.

"You see what you can have? I have much more gold than this—much more. I can buy you houses the like of which you have never before seen in your life. I can buy you dresses and diamonds. You hear me? Such gold like this I can spread out before your feet like a carpet. You hear me?"

A foolish, incredulous smile spread over my mother's face.

"I will give your child everything that is best and most beautiful. I will give her whatever I give my own. I will give her more. Don't laugh. My children have a little cart drawn by a little pony. I will give your child two ponies. My children have a servant. I will give your child one. Hear me. I am a rich man and respected. If you do not believe me, come only with me to Philadelphia and take with you your best friend. Learn and find out about me."

By this time, however, the little man from Philadelphia lost the thread of his argument and began to be repetitive. It was as if he was so amazed at the length of his speech that he forgot what he had already said.

If my mother feared his intentions, he would marry her right in New York and then she could go back with him to Philadelphia and find out if he was a liar or was his mouth pure. What did my mother know what good things lay in a child? Did she know that with the right learning, a child could grow up to be anything? Everything?

For answer, my mother suddenly drew up the blinds.

The little man hastily gathered his gold into the dirty sock, wrapped the entire hoard into the dirty handkerchief, and then straightened his dirty cotton tie.

"I tell you this one thing," he said earnestly before leaving, "that you have just sent away the only man in the world who could have made you fortunate. If you change your mind, I will gladly come back for you. You hear me? I will gladly come back for you."

The door had hardly closed upon him when my mother turned to Mrs. Taub with that same foolish smile I had noted on her face during the man's proposal.

"He must have given his wife a lot of trouble," my mother observed with a great show of wisdom on her expressive face. "It is only when a man feels that he has injured his first very much that he can talk like that to the next woman."

My mother tossed her head and smiled.

That night I saw her serve supper with real tenderness to the rustic looking pants presser. He was our latest boarder. He had oily black hair that parted irregularly on the side. His face was red with sores that lay beneath his skin. His nose was straight but thick. He mouth was straight but thick. His eyes were red and thick and his complaint was always of aching fingers. He was the least offensive of our boarders.

My mother inquired after the state of his sore finger and applied a poultice to it while a customer who had left a skirt to be repaired tapped her feet impatiently and vowed she would never bring another piece of sewing to my mother. No—not if my mother were the last dressmaker on earth!

But my mother smiled at the pants presser.

The man from Philadelphia was forgotten in the trouble that dogged us for three days. Little Frieda had lost her situation and had come to stop with us again until she found a new one. One afternoon a lady elaborately hatted—obviously a lady—called on my mother. She spoke of some sewing, saying that she had been recommended by friends. My mother, always credulous, except in the case of the Philadelphia suitor, listened to her and they talked about sewing. Frieda sat nearby clad in her wrapper (she had not found her corset that morning either). The woman turned to her.

"Do you want a place?" she asked Frieda. Frieda was mildly interested for she had been out of employment for only two days.

"I guess Frieda would. She is a very good cook and cleans like twenty." My mother interposed for Frieda, spurred on by the girl's listless attitude.

"I should want you to be a waitress in my mother's house. Hers left her yesterday," said the lady. The talk centered around wages, days off, the number of members in the family. Then the lady turned to my mother and said, "I guess you had better make some new aprons for Frieda. I will give you the money for the material and pay you right now for the work."

My mother nodded and took the money.

The next day she was summoned to appear in court. She was accused of serving as an employment agent without a license. The apartment was strangely still as she left. Some girl who was with us, I forgot her name, cooked the supper and I helped clean. When I asked the girl why my mother was gone for the whole day, she told me to mind my business.

"Go bury your head in the books," she said to me. "That's all you'll ever be good for."

I skipped into the snow-covered street to meet some friends with whom I was going to track a favorite teacher to her home. I had learned that she walked home and had confided my secret to some hardy souls.

When I returned home, my head filled with visions, I found my mother, blue lipped, sitting at the sewing machine as if stunned. Around her head was a vinegar-soaked cloth.

"At this very machine that woman said, 'Here is money to make aprons,' and I took the money from her and now they want to put me in prison for it." When she saw me, she began to cry. "Are you hungry? Did you get something to eat?"

I shook off her hand. It did not fit in with my mood. I assured her I was all right.

"Where were you all day?" I asked her curiously. She had had to go to a lady who was very sick. She would have to go tomorrow, too. Perhaps she would have to stay for a month—a year or ten years.

My mother was so impressed with the fear of courts that for months afterwards when the name of a court was mentioned she turned pale. She was fined fifteen dollars, which she paid, wondering dully what wrong she had committed.

My mother was in love with the pants presser. I heard her talking to her neighbor, Mrs. Taub.

"When I feel his little finger, I tremble. If that is not love,

28

what is? Yet he, he does not even look at me. I give him his supper and make him little extra dishes and I don't even get a 'thanks.' Everybody sees how I'm growing thin for love of him, but he—he could be blind for all he sees."

I was much too disgusted to protest. My disgust grew to indifference. I was more interested in the difference between Jews and Krishts, and why had I not been born a Krisht when the Krisht was obviously more to be envied.

In all the books I had read, in school and from the library, from the book that had the twins as their complementary heroes, to the L.T. Meade series, to *Little Women,* even to the fairy stories, the people were all Krishts. No Jews were mentioned, therefore where it was not stated, I assumed that they were all Krishts.

I had joined a sewing club in the building where the kindergarten I had attended was located. There I noticed that our "sweet" directress, Miss Mendelsohn, although she had a Jewish name acted like a Krisht—"refined" and wore gloves. Her friends that came down to the club from time to time were all Krisht—and when they weren't they were like her, refined and also wore gloves. I had heard of a club in the Clarke House on Rivington Street where one could go Tuesday evenings and get any book to read—any book that one wished to read. There were all kinds of fairy books procurable I could never borrow from the public library. I went there and found a gentle-voiced Krisht who gave you a book to read and told you strange, simple stories that you learned came from the Bible. Others came from a fairy book and still others from the lady's head.

By dint of close observation I had made up the main difference between Krisht and Jew. Whereas the one wore gloves, the other did not; whereas one always had clean nails, the other had not; whereas the one never argued about paying children's fare on the trolley, the other always did; whereas one spoke perfect English, using long words whose meaning was difficult to render, the other did not.

I decided one twilight upon the all-important step of becoming a Krisht, and so I cried at the parting that would necessarily take place between my mother and myself. My mother coming into the kitchen found me there and lit the gas in dismay.

"Why, what are you crying for?" she asked. "It hurts you some thing?"

I shook my head and sobbed harder. "I want to be a Krisht."

"What? You?" my mother shrieked.

"Yes, I wanna be good! I wanna be a Krisht."

My mother pressed her lips together and regarded me sorrowfully. Then she sputtered. "I'll give you what you want in a minute."

"If you hit me for a hundred years, I won't care," I informed her, suddenly feeling that I had become a martyr. "I wanna be a Krisht. I'm a Krisht anyway. You remember Martha? The Krisht girl who lived next door to the Peckachas? Well, she took me to a church and she made me a Krisht. She made a cross on my back and she spilled water on me." By this time I was overcome by the enormity of the fact that I was already a Krisht and had quite forgotten.

"I'm a Krisht!" I howled. "I'm a Krisht. I'm gawna be good."

My mother began to cry with me out of sheer perplexity.

"What shall I do with her?" she remarked to the rustic-looking pants presser.

"Call a doctor for her," he said in his level voice. He had a soft speaking voice and could sing in a girlish soprano.

I stopped long enough in my frenzied weeping to say, "You go to hell."

He turned his back on me. "I'd give her a licking she'd remember for the rest of her life," he said in louder tones than I had ever heard him use before.

My mother stared at him, astonished. "Oh no, I never hit Bella," she said, but her face looked happier than I had seen it a long time. It pleased her to have the man she was in love with take an interest in her affairs. It encouraged her to believe that perhaps he might return her worship a little.

"Oh, I never hit Bella." And my mother placed a trembling hand upon the pants presser's arm.

A yellow-eyed boy lived next door to us. He was neither son, cousin, nor nephew in the household. There was also a younger girl, and another younger boy who occupied the same anomalous position. There were a lot of men and only one woman, a fat blond who lisped and talked in Russian most of the time.

One day I was informed by the boy that their whole apartment was filled with dolls. I didn't believe him and said so.

"C'm on in an' see," the boy said to me. I have a faint recollection of his colorless face and his mean, little yellow eyes.

I went in.

There were rows and rows of dolls in their boxes and out of their boxes. They were piled against the walls and on the table and chairs. My heart seemed to stop beating at the sight of one dark-eyed doll who had an old rose ostrich feather in her straw hat. She was splendidly attired. She was a lady.

"Oh, I wish I had that doll," I murmured.

"Gimme a kiss, I'll give you the doll," the boy said. He attempted to grasp my shoulders but I eluded him. I ran down the stairs. On the ground floor I found myself trapped by the little fellow, dancing around, his yellow eyes gleaming out of his tallow-colored face.

The door leading to the yard and the skylight was open and I headed for it. I ran in the direction of the yard but he outran me and I had to back into the skylight. I tried to duck under his arm, but he caught me up against the whitewashed wall.

"Lemme alone," I pleaded.

"I ain't doin' nuthin' to yuh," the boy said in assumed grievance. I thought he was off his guard and made a sudden rush past him, but he caught me. And this time he held my arms tight.

"Whaddya wan' from me?" I begged. "Please lemme alone."

The boy searched my face with his lips, his hands gripping my arms so hard that I began to cry. Heretofore I had not used my feet. It wasn't fair to kick when you were fighting with your fists. But I struck out against his shins and the boy let out a howl of pain. By landing another well-aimed blow at his stomach, I made my escape.

The dolls mysteriously disappeared after a day or so and so did the curious unrelated family next door.

I hid while the moving went on. I was afraid of the yellow-eyed boy.

My mother in an unguarded moment told me later that the group next door were a band of thieves and that the little boy was a waif they had picked up and were training.

I forgot him in my new friendship with two little girls named Celia and Pearlie Pechter. They always wore the same kind of dresses, aprons, and hair ribbons and were similarly sweet-natured and anxious to be my subjects. Both bit their fingernails. I planned and executed an elaborate amateur performance for them to admire, inviting the boys and girls from the next yard if they would not break seltzer bottles in the yard— the usual way of guests in returning the impromptu hospitality of the host. They came and the janitor's boy kept order. The end came not with an offensive of the inhabitants of the next yard, but with the offensive of a cranky old lady who lived next door to us. She emptied a pail of water on our heads and brought up to herself a volley of English oaths taken directly, literally, and unmercifully from the Yiddish.

When Celia and Pearlie moved to East Third Street and invited me to come and see their home, especially their bathroom, I knew that this was their response to the entertainment I had given in their honor.

It was a much larger tenement than mine with wider staircases and six tenant families to a floor. When I got halfway upstairs I sensed that something was happening. It inspired me with a feeling that I could not understand, a vague, sorrowful, uneasy feeling.

My two friends met me on their floor and told me in whispers that a woman had died upstairs and that today was the funeral. The three of us sat down on the stairs and talked of it. Celia and Pearlie had heard that the dead woman was very young and that she had just gotten married and that there was a very little baby left over.

Suddenly there was a shriek and a babel of voices on the floor above us. We rose and ran up the stairs. Surrounding a coffin covered by a black velvet coverlet with the sign of the five-pointed star on it were a group of women tearing their hair and beating their breasts. One very old woman threw herself face down upon the coffin and talked to it.

I felt as if the corners of my forehead were receding to the back of my head while with each word that bereft mother uttered a knifelike wave of sympathy swept through my body. The three of us cried.

After the coffin was taken down to the hearse, amid a deal of clatter, an awful stillness settled down upon the halls. We seated ourselves on the stairs and talked of death. Did it really mean that you never saw the dead person again? That if you died, you never could live again?

It was perplexing. We sighed and began all over again.

I spied a moth that was dizzily flying about in feeble circles.

"Look on that white fly," I cried to my two friends. They followed the direction of my finger. "That's the woman's soul. That's her inside."

My friends regarded me questioningly.

"It's what can't be buried," I explained wildly and vaguely. "It's what makes you laugh or cry and love people and hate people. It's—it's feeling and thinking and—it's what can't be put in the ground."

The moth suddenly dropped to the window ledge without a single struggle.

At the same time, a piercing cry cut the silence.

We didn't know where it came from, and my curious, disjointed talk had not been without its effect. We ran into the apartment and shut the door tight.

My friends' mother, who was going to have another baby soon, was tasting something that was boiling on the stove.

"You should take your little brother along when you go on the street," she said without looking up. Neither Celia nor Pearlie made any reply. Their mother looked up suspiciously.

"What's the matter with you?" Observing their frightened glances— "Anybody done you something?"

My friends told her what I had related to them about the white fly. During the recital, I remember the peculiarly slow tightening of her lips and the suspicious narrowing of her eyes—that together with the smell of frying onions. And then, "Go out from here you—you liar, you harlot—you, you're no better than your mother. You hear me, get out from here. Don't you ever show your face in my house again. Go already, you nothing."

I met those two little girls on the corner near the school a few days later. They just looked at me and ran. The smile I tried to give them turned into a stupid parting of the lips and the tears came into my eyes.

I was in the fourth grade in school when I forsook my books for a short but intensively lived period. I gave all my studious friends and subjects to understand that their company was not necessary to my well-being. In other words, I was "mad" on them.

None of them understood. Some did not care; others cared enough to find out the reason for my curious action. They reported to those who did not care that I was a member of a gang of "toughs" on Columbia Street. "Toughs" was the ghetto's name for girls who played with boys. Such girls usually wore pleated skirts that ended above the knees, pinned their ribbons to exploit sheen and breadth, rolled their eyes, sang questionable parodies of popular songs, parodies whose source I have never yet been able to trace. During my novitiate, I learned one to the tune of "Where the River Shannon Flows" that told the sad story of a girl's downfall with intimate details and Sunday School interpolations. It was really a highly moral song, but the girls always giggled when they sang it and added suggestive gestures. I was amazed at their fund of knowledge on all subjects and the way they filched money from their mother's handkerchief knots. For our leader, Mamie Zwerlinger, I had nothing but gaping astonishment. It was through her constant reiteration of the word "deny" in her quarrels with other girls that I included that word in my vocabulary.

"Kin you deny what you told Sadie Farkash?" Mamie would ask, her face so close to her victim's that one could see her reflections in the other's eyes. "Kin you deny it? Let's see yuh try it!"

Mamie was three years older than myself and always called me "Inn'cent." She was flat-faced with ruddy patches on her cheeks, and a flat broad nose that quivered when she was on the war path. She had kinky black hair that she wore straight back from a low, narrow forehead. One day she met the "gang" with an addition to her usual headdress—a bang that reached down to her eyes. She had brought a pair of scissors with her, knowing that her satellites would follow her fashion. Four of them did. The rest said they would ask their mothers first.

I refused with profuse apologies and Mamie gave me one of her famous looks. It consisted of almost closing her large black eyes and drawing up her lips until they almost touched her nostrils. It was a look calculated to strike shame into the hearts of all cowards.

For a time I was sure that my goody-goody friends were all wrong about the boy part of my new acquaintances. But the time came when I was disillusioned. There was a deal of furtive conference between Hattie and Mamie. Hattie was Mamie's lieutenant, blond, long-nosed, and plump, and the gang was told that we were going for a walk to Delancey Street.

"I'm not gawn on the bridge," I announced in a small voice.

I had heard about the Williamsburg bridge. Boys ran after you there and called you names . . . and you had to kiss them.

"Oh, you shut up, Inn'cent. We're not gawna walk on a bridge," Mamie snapped.

We went to Delancey Street and were met by about a half dozen lounging little runts. They were boys. I regarded them closely. This was the sex that was still a secret to me. I grew constrained as I noticed the familiarity that existed between the gang and those boys.

After my introduction as Inn'cent, I became rather anxious that no one whom I knew passed this place. I did not think of my mother's displeasure. She would not have understood why I should have been afraid to be seen in that group. Oh yes, she would have understood the boy part. But it was not the boys I feared, but the girls. It was their easy familiarity with the sex that was so strange to me that made me fear them.

I went home to find my mother already in bed. For a half hour I curbed my desire to ask her to light the gas and let me read for a while. I was almost sick with desire to read a book that told of country and girls—and real boys.

The next day I did not go to Columbia Street but played jacks with Margaret Leizer, the daughter of the butcher who had a store in the tenement. I was entering the fifth game when Hattie passed.

"'lo. Comin'?" she asked.

I gave Margaret her ball and jacks and without a word joined Hattie. We went to Columbia Street. It was hot—stupidly hot.

"You certainly look cool," Hattie assured me as we turned

into Rivington Street. "When 'dya get that bandeau?"*

I told her and she asked me to let her wear it. I let her wear it until we got on Columbia Street and then I asked for its return.

"Stingyguts!" remarked Hattie automatically.

I replaced the bandeau in my hair.

Three of the boys we had met the night before were on the block and a new one, a fourth one. Somehow, I recognized in the new boy what I myself was: an adventurer in friends. I believe he sensed the same thing but we could find nothing to talk about.

Finally, he asked me to play ball with him. He produced a baseball from his pocket. Hattie walked up and a third girl, whose name or face I don't remember, with her. The boy, Archie, scowled at them openly, but the girls chose not to notice.

I can feel the hot sun and see the dry, baked street with its scattering of garbage in the gutter, the walls of tenements rising hopelessly on each side. Archie threw the ball to me. A hump-backed woman crossed between us as I released the ball from my hand. The next moment I was running as fast as I could from Columbia Street, the bandeau in my hand.

This marked the end of my venture into "fast" society.

There was great excitement in the house. My mother and I were going to a wedding. I was to wear a silk dress—white silk with lace—and then we were to go to the bride's house. From there we were to ride in a carriage to the hall on Second Street and Avenue B where the wedding was to take place.

In a carriage!

We were to see the bride before anyone else saw her!

The night before, my mother washed my head in a solution

---

*For those who may not know, a bandeau is shaped like a comb and holds the ribbons in. Place it over the front or back of your head, as you will. —B.S.

of warm water and stale beer, and braided my hair in thin, stiff little plaits that would not let me sleep. This was to make my hair frizzy. In the morning, my head felt as if every hair had been taken out of it, one by one. But the pain was forgotten in the worry I felt; my dress was still unfinished.

At six o'clock, my mother slipped it out from underneath the machine needle with a relieved sigh and expansion of the chest.

"There, cut the cottons off for yourself," she said. "I've got to wash myself."

I cut the threads off and then set the flat iron to heat while I laced my mother's corset for her.

"Not so tight—you must think I'm a stick," my mother said. "You can open your hair while I iron your dress."

I unbraided my "chinky" plaits, my heart making queer jumps as I watched the white silk dress—my white silk dress—come from under the iron in stiff white magnificence. It wasn't a real silk. It was the kind used for linings, a thick material with a silken sheen. But to me it was the material worn by Cinderella at her first ball.

"I'll have to pin it because I have no time to make button-holes," said my mother. "Your hair is combed? Good."

I wore a coat over my silk dress, but that did not hide the lace-edged hem, nor my white stockings and black shoes with white kid tops.

"All dressed up!" sang out Margaret from the milk store.

I turned a sheepish smile in her direction and mentally vowed to "get even" on her.

Arrived at the bride's house, I retired to a corner and watched the bride sitting on a chair, deathly pale. She had had nothing to eat since the night before in accordance with the custom. Her dark eyes shone brightly, however, from underneath the frail white pleats of her veil that descended from the top of her head.

Her dress was more magnificent than mine and her slippers were all satin with little buckles of white glistening beads. A bouquet of pink roses and sprays of lily-of-the-valley rested on the table near her.

In the room, all the three gas jets of the brass chandelier were lit, and grown-up people kept coming up to the bride and going away.

"She stands her fast well," some said.

"Yes, she makes a pretty bride," the others agreed.

When no one was near the bride, I went up and looked at her. She was pretty. She had a little round dent in the tip of her nose.

"Have you come to wish me well too?" the bride asked, pinching my cheek with cold, restless fingers.

In the carriage, I leaned against the lap of the bride and looked out into the street. I could glimpse the envy in the eyes of the children as they caught sight of me almost sitting in the lap of the bride.

My mother sat erect next to the bride, her eyes bright, her nostrils working in a way they had when she wanted to look especially pleasing. She wore a white China-silk waist with very many little tucks and lace insertions in it and a black, pleated voile skirt.

When we got to the hall, there was already a small, substantial crowd waiting at the entrance to watch the bride alight.

In self-conscious pride I preceded the bride. My mother followed and the bride's aunt came next. Then the bride.

A steady color began to stream into her cheeks.

After I had seen the bride seated at the head of the hall, in a kind of throne chair, I noticed that there was another right next to it which remained vacant.

"Who's going to sit in the other chair?" I asked my mother.

"The bridegroom," my mother answered. She was now very happy, for the rustic-looking pants presser had arrived.

"And where is he?" I persisted.

"That's none of your business," my mother said. "Here, I brought you some nuts."

I seated myself on the carpet-covered bench that lined two parallel walls and watched the dancers. The band played waltzes, and the men and women kept turning around and around.

I looked at the lace on my hem. There was a tear in one portion of it.

"I wonder what they did with the bridegroom?"

I got up and smoothed my dress on the sides. I was beginning to be bored. The sight of the whirling figures had been amusing in the beginning.

I could go up and look at myself in the long looking glass in the ladies' dressing room. The women were nursing their babies there. The place smelled like a toilet.

I seated myself on the stairs and began to eat the nuts.

Suddenly, there was a deep quiet and then everyone began gathering in little groups. It seemed to me that someone from above, probably God, had thrown coiled ropes around the people, twisting them around and around—faster and faster until they could do nothing but keep on circling in small groups, breathing out loud long after the ropes were withdrawn.

Presently, I saw a man enter. He looked very important. His bushy brown beard stuck out before him. Everyone turned to stare at him.

Mothers began to search for their children and children to cry out for their mothers.

"Stand next to me," my mother cried.

"What's the matter?" I asked.

"They're going to erect the marriage canopy," she replied happily. She looked furtively at the impassive face of the rustic-looking pants presser.

"So where's the bridegroom?" I asked, my old curiosity returning.

"Sh—sh —" my mother said.

The white lights of the hall suddenly went out and curious little colored lights appeared. At the same time, there was a deal of striking of matches, and the people began to light their little colored candles.

My mother gave me one, already lit, and whispered to me to hold it high. Higher!

A man's voice began to drone, first softly and then louder. At intervals, the voices of younger boys chimed in. Women began to cry. I looked up to see whether my mother was crying too. No, she wasn't, but she was going to. Her nose was slowly reddening and her mouth was beginning to stretch. Clumped in among those grown-ups, I could see nothing. Where was the bridegroom?

I ran out of the oven of warm flesh to the bench that lined the wall and mounted it.

Now I could see!

A man was leading another man around the bride whose face was now entirely covered by the veil. Would he ever stop going round and round?

The sound of breaking glass . . . a din of scrambled voices like the rush of the "L" heard from a distance.

"Come down from there," my mother called. "We will soon eat. The march is beginning."

Indeed, couples were already forming and the music was wheezing away— diddle, diddle, diddle—dummm!

My mother grabbed the rustic-looking pants presser by the arm and me by another and we became a part of the march. Down we marched, and up we marched, in and out and, finally, we marched downstairs to the huge basement dining room where the tables were set and waiting.

First there was fish—boiled, stuffed fish; then chicken soup with round, little eggy things in it; then roast chicken; then cake and tea.

Mothers crammed the mouths of their children with food

and the children ate as if they had been starved for three days. I saw one woman, whose wig had lost a bit of its equilibrium because of the excitement, fill the pockets of her oldest boy with fruits and nuts.

"Why don't you eat?" my mother asked me.

"I'm not hungry," I replied. I must have been sleepy.

"She thinks she is the bride of yesterday," commented the rustic-looking pants presser, pinching my arm. "You hear, a bride fasts for only one day."

We walked home in the chilly, damp hours of early morning.

"Look, she is sleeping already!" my mother said as she guided my fumbling feet. "Well, now we will be able to go and take a bath without worrying about the woman knocking on the door to tell us to get out of the water, somebody else is waiting. . . . She married well. She has three rooms and a bath! Think of that. Biela Chentze's daughter. How many times her mother used to come to our house for food, I should have a thousand dollars for —"

"Carry me!" I begged suddenly.

"Carry you! A big girl like you!" said the rustic-looking pants presser with his soft girlish laugh.

My mother laughed too.

PART II

Stanton Street

S tanton Street has no personality of its own for me. It is just
a street of the East Side for me—not gutterish enough nor
yet clean enough to warrant distinct remembrance.

My recollection has this street bound up with the house we
lived in on the corner of Lewis and Stanton Streets. It was a
unique house. You could come up through the Stanton Street
side and then go out through Lewis Street side or vice versa.
And always there would be the candy store on the corner where
on cold winter nights, I would cajole my mother into buying me
sweet, watery hot chocolate.

There were four apartments in a row on each floor. In the
middle, there was a square, high, wooden fence built around a
hole in the floor so as to permit the light from the roof to give
itself to the kitchens whose single windows faced the hall.

We children used to poise ourselves in the spaces between
the wooden spikes of the fence and spit over and down on the
floor below. Those of us who were too small to reach to the top
would content ourselves by spitting down through the chinks.

Out of our hall, which was quite spacious—we sometimes

danced in it—stretched another—a narrow, lightless strip that always smelled of conscienceless cats.

I spent one year in this house adventuring in friends and religion.

GOD
God.
god.
gOd.
goD.

I wrote these down and then looked earnestly at my mother's back as she sat sewing at the machine. She was singing.

I turned back to my list and added exclamation points.

"Don't sing," I said to my mother.

"Don't listen," my mother replied without turning around.

I took my paper and pencil into the hall. But there was not enough light near the fence so I went over to the stocking peddler's side. A stocking peddler and his family of wife and three daughters lived on the extreme left where light trickled in through an airshaft. In the summer, at times they would all come out into the hall and sit around several small laundry baskets of stockings and examine them for damages and resultant pricings. The father would take the black stockings, the mother, the men's socks; the girls would divide the brown silk stockings and children's socks among themselves.

But the light was just as poor on the stocking peddler's side so I returned to the fence and seated myself on the floor.

"God," I said aloud.

I repeated it.

I thought of the day my mother had sat with one of her countrymen discussing a third person of whom our visitor had said, "He grabs God by the feet but he's not to be trusted with a penny."

God!

Feet!

I had stared at the man as if he had committed murder and waited momentarily for an exhibition of God's wrath. But it did not come, and for days afterward I grew moody over the man's impiety. Even if God had feet, how had he the temerity to mention it?

The man had violated not so much the tenets of the religion around me, as my own private religion that was an odd mixture of superstition, paganism, and myths of my own making—a part of the inchoate thing I called God.

A few examples. I disliked roaches not because they were creeping things and repugnant to the senses but because they destroyed food. And food was good. God wanted us to eat and be healthy.

I disliked washing my head in kerosene oil. It was slimy to the touch, even though the hair did acquire a certain silky sleekness after the ablution. So I imagined, after I had washed my head in the smelly solution and was lying in bed, that the angels sent from God smiled down upon me. They usually stuck their heads through the hall window, because it was cleaner than the narrow one that faced the skylight. Sometimes I substituted the head of a mythical lover. But I felt just as sure that God was pleased with me for having washed my head in kerosene water.

God to me was a Thing who liked to be pleased— a fatherly, formless, vague body whom one should please.

There was the other element: fear, but that played a secondary if important part in my religious fervor.

I crossed out gOd. I didn't like the way it looked. The wooden fence hurt my back. I slumped down until only the back of my head rested against it.

I wondered whether God was angry with me for leading Margaret into temptation. Margaret was a classmate of mine, a truly religious girl whose father was quite a dignitary in the synagogue—something like a trustee—and owned a milk store.

Before sundown on Friday, on my suggestion, Margaret had

put five cents into the corner of her handkerchief. On Saturday afternoon, when we were standing near the flaring boards that marked the entrance to the moving-picture theater, she had looked off into the distance, first at the Williamsburg Bridge (better known on the East Side as the Delancey Street Bridge) and then at the white-flecked sky while I had put my hands into her pocket and drawn out the money in the handkerchief.

Neither of us had questioned the righteousness of our acts, for Margaret had silenced her religious conscience before she had decided to fall, and I had had no compunction whatever. We were complying with the rules of her God, I had argued. I was sinning and she was not.

But somehow sitting in the half light with that list before my eyes and the fence prodding my back, I began to think that perhaps my God wouldn't be pleased at Margaret's defection.

I punctured the edges of the paper with the point of my pencil.

He was probably very sad. Hurt.

I felt the tip of a shoe kick against my upturned sole. I looked up, startled. It was the rustic-looking pants presser.

"What's the matter. Mourning?" he asked in his soft voice.

One night my mother took me to Brooklyn and we sat in a vacant store that was filled with chairs. There were a few people—very few. Sitting on the platform were a few other men and women. One of them was sweet-faced, I remember, and sad. At intervals we rose and sang to the chords that a blond, pink-cheeked, round-shouldered man expelled from a small organ. We sang of Jesus.

I asked my mother why she went there and she laughed. I suspected my mother of not being frank with herself.

I had decided to wait at the Rivington Street Church until I would meet someone who looked as if he could lead me out of my religious maze. I did not choose the synagogue because I could not imagine the bearded Jews entering or emerging from it stopping to talk to a little girl who questioned their faith. Besides, my connection with the synagogue was one of holidays only, as on Yom Kippur and Rosh Hashanah when I would go to see my mother as she wept into her prayer book, sitting on the bench among many other crying, red-nosed women. I felt no everyday kinship with the synagogue. I had an idea that it belonged to the menfolk only.

My decision to wait outside of the church for my leader-out-of-the-wilderness rose from two sources. First, a little girl I had known for a short time had told me that she had gone to a kind of summer play school there and that she had also gotten ice cream and cake on several occasions. No, they hadn't made crosses on her back or her heart. They didn't even say Jesus Christ or make you say Jesus Christ.

And second, I had once seen a man enter that church who had greeted me with patient eyes and soft smile. It had come to me in a flash, then, that that man might perhaps be able to set me straight, religiously speaking.

I did not wait regularly, but each day that the feeling urged me I would hurry down to Rivington and Cannon Streets. And one afternoon, I met him. He greeted me with the same patient eyes and soft smile. I remember him as a tall, slightly stooping man with gray side whiskers.

He would have passed me by, but I held up a wavering, restraining hand. "You want to talk to me?" His voice was melodiously soft and wonderfully pitched.

I don't know how I began telling him of my religious difficulties but I remember asking him why Jews are called Sheenies.

"Sheen means bright," he assured me and I was comforted somewhat.

I told him of the day we had gone to a wedding in Brooklyn and how we had lost our way coming home. We walked for many unfamiliar hostile blocks, my mother, the rustic-looking pants presser (the least offensive boarder), old man Lefkowitz, whose beard almost reached to his bosom, his daughter, Sarah, a blond, cow-eyed girl of twenty who laughed at everything, and myself. Finally we struck a trolley car line. Where that car line led, we did not know. My mother began wishing that someone would pass our way, of whom she could inquire the right direction. Over and over again. . . .

As if in response, several gentile boys—not one more than fifteen—came our way. At the sight of us, they began to snicker and lurch against each other. Before we were aware of what was happening, one of them pulled at the hem of my white cashmere coat while a second seized hold of old man Lefkowitz's beard and made as if to cut it.

A sheepish smile spread over the pants presser's face.

My mother made free with her hands and feet and the boys scattered. Gathered together at a safe distance from us, they began to shout derisively:

"Sheenies, ya damn Sheenies!"

They gesticulated wildly with their hands and mimicked among vile epithets: "For vot? For vot, I esk you?"

Away into the darkness they sped like leering shadows of the night, but the pain they left for me tortured me even after I had received comfort.

"They were not true Christians," observed the man sadly, after I had finished speaking.

At parting, he gave me a dime which I spent on a corned beef sandwich with mustard.

Here at this house, while I was getting religion on and off my mind, I made new friends. Margaret was still coming to see me and I her, but our relations were rather strained. She had asked me for a "fancy pin," a brooch which my mother wore exclusively. She knew this. After a deal of bickering with myself, I told her that I couldn't give her my mother's "fancy pin." Margaret became a little cooler, but I didn't mind. I was ready for a change in friends.

There was a thin little girl, whose narrow chest and large brown eyes had won my compassion. She had a large nose and a very weak little mouth with a tiny chin. Her hair was always sleekly drawn back from her forehead, and she always wore clean ribbons and clean aprons. In my mind there were two kind of girls, the kind who wore clean starched aprons and the kind who didn't. I belonged to the latter class but my friends were recruited from the former.

I liked Dinah very much. She would come on Saturdays and help me clean the sideboard of its lemonade sets and soiled doilies.

She begged to do the washing, but I always refused. She dried much better than I ever could. She was a perfect companion for one who wanted an echo—but I wanted someone to disagree with me, someone who could lead me. So one day I dispatched a note by her sister Becky, saying that I was "mad" on her.

I received a letter back in which Dinah implored me to still remain her friend. What had she done to deserve such treatment? I did not reply and she came to plead her cause. She left in tears, for I had not replied once to her.

I was relieved when she left.

There was May Weiss. I liked May for one reason. She could, by a twist of her tongue, elicit a little shower on any place you indicated. It was a trick worthy of emulation. Since I could not do it myself, I cultivated May. Outside of this sole accomplishment, May was not especially my kind. True, she could play the Fairy Wedding Waltz with a dash and vigor that always won admiring remarks from company, but she could not fool me. I had detected false notes in her playing.

May kept coming to my house at all hours and I was beginning to tire of her attentions. One day, as we sat in the hall, she asked me whether she couldn't wear the same dresses that I wore

. . . the same hair ribbons . . . the same shoes. The request sickened me.

Where was May Weiss's self-respect?

To escape from her pleading little "cat's eyes," I turned away my head. May caught at my hand. I wrenched it away.

But the gods punished me, for I myself was eaten up with admiration for others. One whom I worshiped lived not far from me. Miriam wore her blonde hair in little Egyptian curls all over her head, and at other times, straight with a big plaid ribbon on the top. She had a little, slightly turned-up nose and a fretful little mouth. Her sister gave piano lessons. This fact alone would have given her caste had she been as ugly as she was remarkably pretty. Miriam ruled us all, friends and teachers.

I idolized her. I would offer her everything I had. I would help her in her lessons and in every way I could, especially in her geography. Margaret, she who had cast fond glances at my mother's brooch, helped her with her arithmetic, practically doing everything for her. And Miriam played favorites with us all.

When I watched her dance I would grow sick with love for her. She was so pretty, so graceful—so everything I wanted to be. Sometimes we would sing together; Miriam could harmonize well with me. The song we usually sang was "Sweet Molly Malone." We could sing it fourteen times during the day and never tire.

One day, Miriam took me to the house to show me that she could play the piano with her back turned to it. She did it and then we sang together. As we came out of the house a boy of eighteen rushed by us, out of breath.

"Who's that?" I asked curiously.

"My brother," Miriam said shortly.

The boy's face stayed with me, as if anxious to be located. I knew I had seen him before and I tried to think where. Finally, my thoughts went back to the days we had lived on Cannon

Street . . . little Sadie . . . new lavender dress . . . moving pictures. Oh yes! My mind leapt eagerly upon the memory only to recoil in fear and disgust. No, I did not want to think of the time little Sadie's painted face was streaked with tears.

It sounds sentimental. But wet, painted faces are so poignantly helpless.

The day of the lavender dress started out very happily for Sadie. She had made it with the help of my mother, and when it was finished she could not resist showing it off immediately on the street. It was made in the coat-dress fashion—a straight panel, a shaped waist and a skirt with pleats starting a little above the knees. Sadie was like a child when she was happy. She made me help her pull the narrow black ribbon through the insertion at the neck and sleeves and where the pleats joined the body of the skirt. Then as a reward, she announced that she would take me to the "movies." It was then known as the "nickel show" and if we children came early, we could gain admittance "two for a nickel" and sometimes "two and a baby for a nickel." It depended on the place we patronized.

Sadie and I went to the Victoria Music Hall where moving pictures and Yiddish and English sketches were presented. We were just about to enter when Miriam's brother stepped up to Sadie and suddenly put his mouth to her ear. He did not whisper but voiced his demand so loudly that people passing on the sidewalk stopped to gape. For a moment, I thought Sadie was going to faint. A gray line formed around her mouth. Her eyes closed. When she opened them, she cried out so all who had stopped could hear.

"You dirty, rotten bum!"

At the same time she opened the door to the theater with a vehemence that almost knocked me off my feet and banged it tight behind her.

To my prediction of what Miriam's brother (I did not know then that he was) would do to her, Sadie merely bit her lower lip harder and harder. Then she began to cry. Luckily it was dark. I tried to say something to soothe her but I could not understand. She had been so brave in the beginning. The tears dropped into the lap of her lavender dress.

"To think that such a thing should have happened to me just when I was so happy with my new dress. It ain't right!" she muttered fiercely.

Then she gave herself up determinedly to looking at the screen.

But I could not forget. I plucked at her sleeve until I could feel that she was looking at me. "Supposing he's outside—when we go home?" I offered.

Again Sadie drew in her lips, this time with a decision that added much to my respect for her. "I'll call a policeman," she replied. "Now, shut up. I'm gawna see this picture. Didn't I pay a nickel?"

I tried to smile at her witticism but failed.

When we came out, Miriam's brother was still leaning against one of the billboards, his hands in his pockets, a cynical, loose-lipped smile on his old-young face. As we approached the front of our house, Sadie asked me to look around and see if he was following us.

"Look yourself," I answered and rushed up the stairs.

In the playground one noon (I must have been in the fifth grade), Miriam took me aside and said she wanted to tell me something. She was "busting from laughing," and without cause, childlike. I joined heartily.

"You know what it is?" Miriam asked me. She seemed disappointed.

"No," I shook my head. "Honest, I don't."

Miriam began to laugh again uncontrollably.

"Hurry up," I said, "the bell'll ring."

She took me to a farther corner and told me a conundrum whose answer had something to do with the nuptial night.

Miriam finished and waited expectantly for my applauding laugh, but I merely stared stupidly at her.

"What's the matter with you?" she demanded irritably, prodding me in the side. "Why don't you laugh?"

The bell saved me from replying. I don't know what I should have said to Miriam if it had not.

I swung to the other extreme in the choice of my next friend. Edith was uniformly unobtrusive. She was happiest when inconspicuous. Her whole bearing was as indicative of this as was her soft, low-pitched voice.

Edith Felk had a low, broad, slightly bulging forehead—the more since her mother believed in drawing every strand of hair tightly into two braids at the back. Then her two wide gray eyes set far apart always looked at one with such queer one-sided intensity that I could swear at times that Edith was cross-eyed. She was not. It was the effect of her inward vision. Because we were as unlike temperamentally and physically as could be, our friendship took a long time to assert itself.

For a time Edith could only visit me. Her mother, a rigorously religious woman, did not know whether to admit me to her home. She capitulated finally and I became a frequent visitor at the house. Besides Edith, there was Mary, an older girl who was downright ugly, but whose thick brown hair fell down to her knees; two silent, older boys, who always appeared to be harboring some grudge that they could not get rid of, and three younger children. It was a decidedly silent house—and more so on Friday and Saturday when religious observance forbade everything that would tend to introduce noise. On Friday before sundown, the four girls of the family would comb their hair, the mother helping the youngest who had to wear hers in curls. Before going to bed each would draw a cap over the freshly combed and plaited hair. In the morning, the cap was removed but no comb touched the hair until Sunday morning.

Gravely and quietly Edith explained the reason for this

process. The hair might break while being combed. In that case, the child sinned for having torn something on the Sabbath.

I could not help snickering. "Supposing the rubber band in the cap busts when you're sleeping. Is it a sin too?" I queried wickedly. Edith, sweet-natured, did not take offense but tried very hard to mold her mournful mouth into a smile.

My friendship with Edith is one of the truly beautiful things I have to look back upon. And yet our relations consisted simply of going to the library together, to school together, and sometimes doing our lessons together. I liked doing my lessons in Edith's house. There was the quiet that I had come to welcome as a blessed relief to the noise that always seemed to infest our house. At night the Felks used candle and lamplight, and that too made it restful.

Adventures Edith and I never met, but we both had fertile imaginations. Together we would weave tales of startling episodes, and Edith's gray eyes would recede under her brows and become far away in their vision.

We visited every public library in the section and far beyond when we learned that our cards were transferable. Seward Park Branch, Tompkins Park Branch, Bond Street Branch, Rivington Street Branch, and the Second Avenue Branch saw us both, eyes alight.

It is a tradition, I suppose, among all the bookworms of eleven and twelve on the lower East Side that one public library at one time in its life is superior to the other in having available particular kinds of books. For instance, the Tompkins Park Branch had all the Gypsy Breynton series; the Bond Street Branch the Hildegarde books; and the Second Avenue or Ottendorfer Branch all the Patty series.

Edith and I found this out and would traipse all over the city in search of say, *The First Violin*. Sometimes one of us would be left on guard at one branch where it would be likely that *The First Violin* would be on the shelves later in the day. Most of the time we worked together. We would curve our bodies and bob our heads every which way when a girl who looked as if she might have a "good" book came to exchange it for another. Sometimes it would be the book we wanted, and then it would behoove me, as the older of the two, to step up to the astounded "teacher's" back and say, "Please, could we have that book?"

The librarian's back would stiffen. She was by this time stamping another group of books.

"What book?" she would snap.

"The book the girl brought back—the girl with the blue ribbon."

Edith would be sibilantly whispering the name of the book to me, frantic with anxiety.

"The book's name is *The First Violin,* by Fothergil," I would repeat from Edith's hurried prompting.

If the line stopped here, and there were no more books to stamp, the librarian would relax her back and give us the book. Then there would be exultation in our camp. Usually all the way home we would say nothing to each other. Sometimes our good fortune would be unparalleled and we would get two books we had been hankering for these three weeks and more. Then, all we would do was to look into each other's eyes and burst out into hysterical lilts of laughter.

But I grew tired of having to wait for the books we wanted from one day to another and I decided to join another library so as to have a second card. Edith when she heard shook her head obstinately. No, she wouldn't do that. It was wrong.

"But how is it wrong?" I argued with her. "What does a lib'ary care if you have a hundred cards, so long as you don't tear or dirty the books?"

Edith admitted the sanity of my arguments but refused to join me. So it was I alone who got the first typewritten letter we had ever seen. It had the letterhead of the New York Public Library, and it addressed me as Dear Madam. Me, Dear Madam!

Edith read the letter over. She was duly impressed by the regard the New York Public Library showed for me by its salutation, but being a little more practical than I, she immediately acquainted me with the facts.

"You can belong only to one lib'ary," she announced with the air of one who has scored a point, "it says so in this letter."

"But what's the diff'rence?" I demanded.

"It says so in the letter," repeated Edith.

"But anyway I got out books on the second card," I could not help saying.

"Yes, but you can't do it any more," Edith gently insisted.

"They can't arrest me if I do," I hazarded boldly.

Edith was silently weighing this new angle. "How do you know?" she asked without any particular emphasis on any word.

I lapsed into silence.

Suddenly we looked at each other and burst into laughter. "Dear Madam!"

Just about the ages of ten and twelve, and even much more before them, there burns brightly in every ghetto child's brain the desire to see what lies without the ghetto's walls. For there are very definite high walls on all sides of us. Edith and I had already walked as far as Second Avenue and Third Street— which was quite a distance from Lewis and Stanton Streets, but we had always stifled the wish to go on further. I had once been lost when I was about six following a May party to Seventh Street Park. And I had been taken to 14th Street by my mother who had bought me a coat there.

For a week, Edith and I talked much of Paris, California, Coney Island, the country, London, and Fifth Avenue before we finally decided that we would walk to Andrew Carnegie's home. I don't know how we happened to hit on the residence of the late steel king, but we had heard that it was on Madison Avenue and Sixty-seventh Street.* We were first to go to the

---

*In fact, Carnegie's mansion stood at Fifth Avenue and Ninety-first Street. It is now the home of the Cooper-Hewitt National Museum of Design. —R.L.

library and then to "rubberneck" Andrew Carnegie's home.

That Saturday, Edith and her sister and I landed at Greenhut-Siegel's Department Store on Fourteenth Street— just to rest. As soon as we found ourselves there, we began to wander around on the main floor. We could merely stare . . . the ribbons, the silk petticoats, the ladies' lace jabots, the perfumes and powders. We could merely stare at the circular candy counter that surrounded the fountain. In the midst of the fountain was a huge figure of a woman that shone like gold. Its belly, we concluded, must be filled with candy.

When the moving stairs gripped our eyes, we could do nothing but advance toward them in a trance. We boarded them, icy with fear. We had never before been on escalators. The sensation, after a while, proved exceedingly pleasant. We looked at each other with congratulating eyes. We decided to "do" the rest of the building on the moving stairs. On the third or fourth floor, we decided to take an elevator and go down—but here Edith and Mary objected. That would be riding.

"Moving stairs is riding," I suggested wickedly.

"No," replied the gentle-voiced Edith. "The stairs move but they can't ride."

We walked down to the main floor and began our Jacob-like ascendancy. All went well until we reached the third floor where a man in uniform grabbed us by the arms.

"You just walk yourselves down and get out o' here just as quick as you know how," he said. "If I see you here again, I'm gawna have you arrested." He frowned threateningly.

We giggled.

On the main floor again, we regarded each other stoically and decided to continue our walk to Andrew Carnegie's house. Outside, however, we found that it was nearly five and Edith and Mary demurred. They had to be present at the havdalah ceremony which takes place in every Jewish home on Saturday at sundown. It consists of pouring a little brandy or wine on the table and lighting it with a special kind of braided candle. Then each would sip of the remainder. The prayer is one that falls under the heading of holy differentiations.

As we got nearer home, we could barely exchange good-nights. Each of us had received an insult in the presence of the other; also we were tired and disappointed. We had not seen Andrew Carnegie's home, and we knew despite earnest protestations to the contrary that we would never attempt to walk to it again.

But the moving stairs had been a discovery!

Helen was another of my brief flames. She had a small, very dark pointed face and little black curls to which she usually added a red ribbon. When we girls quarreled with her, we called her Pennyface. Her father owned the thriving candy store on the corner. Since she had a stepmother, I forthwith presented her with my pity although there was no need for it. Her stepmother was a very kind, hopelessly fat young woman with deep-set blue eyes and rough black hair that stood out about her head as if she had just arisen from bed.

Helen was several years older than myself and had already read *Tess of the D'Urbervilles.* She had renamed it "Tess of the Dumpyvilles." On her prompting, I had read it, but I am afraid I did not understand it very well—all except "Out of the frying pan into the fire." It made no lasting impression on me except that I felt Tess had not been given a square deal.

The thing that attracted me to Helen was that she was causing a young man to suffer. He was sixteen and was already in his third year of high school. I saw him trying to make her listen to him one night. He was well built but curiously short-legged, partly because of their tendency to go outward at the knees. He wore glasses and spoke like a gentleman. But Helen did not want to listen to him and walked away in the middle of his speech.

I felt matronly sympathy for that boy for I was in the throes of a domestic attack. My mother had been taken sick one day and it fell upon me to purchase the fish, the vegetables, and chicken. When my mother was better I still continued going to Delancey Street Bridge Fish Market where I would with a dexterous movement of my finger lift up the gills to see whether the fish had red blood. Besides that, I who had always scorned any kind of needlecraft began to knit a cape.

I scrubbed my three floors dutifully every Friday, although my mother didn't think I should. She sensed it wouldn't last however and so let me have my own way. It did not, but while my domestic fervor lasted, my sympathy for Helen's high school boy was acute and deep.

On Friday nights, I would meet all the girls—Helen and Fanny Rapp, whom we facetiously called Fanny-Rap-Me-in-the-Eye, May Weiss, and two or three others whom I can't recall—and we would engage in a screaming game of tag called "Help." Sometimes it would be Chinese Tag and sometimes it would be "Colors" or "Did you find a rat in your milk today?" Frequently, we would vary these games by daring bits of mischief. One of us would innocently approach a passerby and ask how to get to Cannon Street. The man or woman, if a stranger to this innocent trick, would seriously stop and explain. The asker would listen just as seriously, but the rest of us would be huddled together rocking or pinching each other with glee.

"She's fooling you, mister!" another of us would suddenly shout. And the man would go on his way, cursing us audibly for wasting his time and credulity.

In the case of a woman, one of us would step up to her and say in a shy whisper, "Missus, you're losing your petticoat!"

The woman—she was usually hatted, for we knew a bareheaded woman did not always care about such matters—would then run swiftly to the nearest hallway to correct her refractory apparel.

As soon as she was out of sight, we would burst out into hilarious laughter.

Other means of spending our Friday evening time would be

to settle ourselves comfortably into a corner of a store doorway or on empty milk cans and sing school and street songs. I sustained the second part indiscriminately called tenor or alto during these impromptu recitals. Afterwards, I would be called on to render my imitations of my teachers or of a woman buying a pair of stockings on the street, or I would tell melodramatic tales of adventure, disguised thinly as dreams.

Later in the evening, Helen and I would naturally draw away from the rest and seat ourselves on the little stone doorstep in front of the watch and clock repair shop. And Helen would talk of her high school boy.

One night I assured her that if she continued in her heartless fashion the high school boy would forget her.

"Well, I don't believe in 'stick to me kid, you'll get diamonds,'" Helen replied with a birdlike flirt of her head.

I had never heard that phrase before and asked Helen to repeat it. I said it after her word for word and then we both said it together with individual intonations. For no reason, we both commenced laughing without ceasing, trying our best to say connectedly, "Stick to me kid, you'll get diamonds."

A family living next door included a very old woman and a very old man, several grown children and several young ones—the youngest a girl of my own age. If she had not been white, she would have been easily taken for a Negro girl. So she was called Niggerte. My interest did not lie in her—she was too servile and at the same time displayed a certain obstinacy at times that was not to my liking. I kept up an appearance of pleasure in her company for the sake of getting information, an inkling of which had kindled my imagination.

Her older sister, who had been abandoned by her husband for another woman, was trying to get him back by magic. I had heard my mother talking of midnight ceremonies wherein candles and mirrors figured extensively. I was anxious to know more. I'm afraid the Niggerte was stupid, for to all of my questions, delicate or straightforward, she would shrug her shoulders and elevate her thick lips. "I dunno," she would say.

"You're a dope," I finally told her one day and gave her up entirely.

One day, the eldest sister came in to talk to my mother.

As usual, I had a book before my eyes. To my mother, that was proof enough that my ears were not functioning.

They talked in whispers. I could barely hear them, as now and then my mother would set the wheel of the sewing machine going. She stopped suddenly, started, and rose excitedly. "But you know, you mustn't," she cried.

The eldest sister nodded and her sullen face grew dark and bitter. "Don't worry, I didn't. I remembered in time," she assured my mother with the smile of a cynic. Her face was one of those pointed sallow kinds that never fatten even with the best of foods. She had the weariest brown eyes that I had ever seen and I felt very sorry for her. (I have since seen eyes to which hers might have been likened to wedding lights.)

My mother set her work aside and gave herself up to listening to the eldest sister. I, likewise, but unnoticed, put my book down. It seems that through a friend the eldest sister had reached a woman who practiced witchcraft, a not uncommon practice, especially mimetic magic, on the lower East Side. To her she had told the story of her husband's desertion and her subsequent failures to locate him. The witch (I called her that then) had given her nine candles, one of which she was to light every midnight for nine days. She was to set the candle before the mirror and stand in front of it naked. She was to call the name of her husband three times and watch the mirror.

If she screamed, she would go crazy.

"My teeth wanted to tear at each other," wailed the eldest sister, "but I held myself in. I didn't scream but the tears came to me. I saw him, Fanny, I saw him the second night. He was getting out of bed and was dressing. But when I stopped calling, he went back to sleep. I saw it in the looking glass. Oh, he looked so bad as if he had come out of the ground. He is drinking. I know. I can do nothing. I can't hold him back from his devils."

If the eldest sister wanted her husband to come to her that same night, the witch told her to go down to the edge of the water—that would have been the pier of the East River—and turn a rock over and call his name out loud. Her husband would come to her that night from whatever place he happened to be in at the time.

"But I'm afraid. If someone could go with me, I would not be afraid so much, but nobody can come with me. That's what makes it so terrible." The eldest sister began to wipe her eyes. I do not know when she ceased crying during those nine days.

My mother comforted her in the sympathetic way she had.

"It's only two days more," she assured the woman.

"I wish I were dead," returned the eldest sister.

There was a baby's weak cry and she rose. "I stayed home from the shop on account of her," she said. "She is so sickly. She's always crying. Her head doesn't move from the hole it made in the pillow. Oh God, how much longer will you plague me?"

Such an exit could not fail but arouse me—but strangely enough it was only the part of me that loved the melodramatic. I was too young to feel any real pity for the eldest sister.

From the Niggerte I managed to elicit enough to fill the gaps in my story. The little baby's name was Mirele and because her grandmother, the Niggerte's mother, disliked the noise, the eldest sister had had to leave her in the nursery on Cannon Street. During the night the baby had improved a little and so the eldest sister had gone to work (she was a tacker on men's coats) and brought the baby to the nursery.

Last night had been the eighth night. Tonight would be the ninth. Would the husband come back? I lay back on my side of the bed and imagined the eerie scene: the nude woman standing in front of the mirror, a single candle flickering in the dark—and then the little moving picture in the mirror.

I longed to keep awake until after midnight but I could not. It was not necessary. At two o'clock in the morning, we were awakened by a loud rapping on the wall. For a moment, we could not locate it. I felt my mother breathing hard next to me. The rapping commenced again, this time accompanied by a loud wail that was recognized as that of the eldest sister.

"My baby is dead. People, my baby is dead!"

My mother slipped out of bed, cautioning me not to move out of it until she came back. The wailing rose higher and higher and then died down gradually. I fell into a semi-slumber, and then a shriek louder than I had ever heard before seemed to throw down the wall that separated our bedroom from that of the eldest sister.

"Now you're already here! He's here. He's here. Look on him. Here he is. Oh, my baby is dead. And my husband is back. God gives and God takes."

"God gives and God takes," settled down into the mourner's chant and lulled me back to sleep.

PART III

Lewis Street

L ewis Street has the same north and south boundaries as Cannon, running parallel to it as it does.

The part of it which has to do with me stretches between Stanton and Houston beginning at Stanton with a little, musty, low-ceilinged drugstore and a gilt-edged, palatial saloon and ending at Houston with a tiled, high-ceilinged drugstore and a grocery store opposite it.* Halfway between the little drugstore and the butter and egg store was the butcher shop in whose window lung and calves' livers were displayed. On Saturdays, the window was bare except for a few large imprisoned flies and sheets of newspaper hanging from the spikes by one corner.

In the house next to ours lived Birdie, who loved a vaudeville ventriloquist, and a tough guy whose father spanked him on the street to break his spirit. I remember these two vividly.

---

*The length of Lewis Street today is much curtailed. It runs only from Grand Street north to the Williamsburg Bridge, one short block. Bella Spewack's haunts now lie below the Baruch Houses. —R.L.

The snow on this street turned black on the second day. The rain became mud immediately.*

I was now twelve and acutely conscious of the sordidness of the life about me. To escape, I hid behind my books and built up a life of my own in the public school I attended on East Broadway and at the settlement house on Madison Street.

These were more real to me than my home or the street.

My mother and the boarder with whom she was in love did not exist for me as vividly as did Queen Guinevere or my piano teacher with her long neck and her long fingers. She had a way of throwing her head back and frowning when she played.

My piano teacher was mine only for four months; at the end of that time she eloped with a sandy-haired gentile she had met at a "sociable." The street was alive with that scandal for days, but on the third day it learned that Birdie, who loved the ventriloquist, was slowly dying of tuberculosis.

In the summer, the street talked on its stoops. In the winter, it talked in hallways and more briefly in airshafts. It rarely whispered. That was not the way of the Street.

To me, Lewis Street with its figures was like a badly painted backdrop against which the people of my books, school, and settlement played the most important roles. Sometimes the people of my backdrop exchanged places with these, and then I drew back and hid until the backdrop was itself again.

At school, there was first the assembly period when doors rolled back and mediocre schoolrooms became a vast auditorium. You marched in with your class holding yourself straight and stiff, turning square corners with military exactitude. You looked out furtively from beneath your lashes to see if your teacher, now playing the march on the piano, noticed that your shoulders were back and your stomach in.

---

*Not all the streets of Manhattan were paved. —R.L.

You stood up and saluted the flag:

> "I pledge allegiance to my flag
> And to the Republic for which it stands
> One nation indivisible —"

And then you gulped:

> "With lib-urrr-ty and justice forall!"

And then you sat down and listened to the principal read the Bible. It would take years to read the Bible without skipping, you decided. Years. But there was a lot of conversation in it. And you never wanted to skip that. Never.*

Lilly Hirsch wears a new apron, the threads still hanging from the shoulders. She looks at you self-consciously. You look away. You have no apron on. Just a soiled, blue serge dress. You feel your inferiority, but you don't care. You can beat Lilly at grammar with your eyes closed. You can beat her at history. You can beat her in g'ography. . . . You resolve that tomorrow you will wear a white apron even if your mother has a million pleated skirts to sew.

"And they shall know that I am the Lord their God that brought them forth out of the land of Egypt that I may dwell among them: I am the Lord their God," droned the principal.

He shut the big book and you sang: "Praise God from Whom all blessings flow."

You sang the alto, although you weren't supposed to. You tried to stop yourself, but you couldn't.

---

*Bible readings—always from the Old Testament—were a standard feature of New York City school assemblies at least through World War II. Although the readings may have alienated some students and teachers, the virtue of endlessly exposing the children—many from non-English speaking homes—to the rolling cadences and language of the King James's translation may well have compensated for what civil libertarians view today as a breach of the Constitutional separation of church and state. —*R.L.*

And then the principal got up again and said, "Today we are going to have some recitations from 7A-3. Sophie Leschnitzky."

On Arbor Day, you had a long piece all by yourself. About trees being planted and giving shade. Where were all those trees? you wondered.

Anyway, Arbor Day was a wonderful day.

Too soon, the recitations were over and your teacher struck a chord. That meant get up. A second chord. Face right. And then the march began again and you once more became stiffly erect and turned right angles. You wondered whether your teacher at the piano could see that your shoulders were back and your stomach was in.

During the vacation, I spent all the time that I could reading in the public library near Seward Park. In the evening, I skated. Frequently girls of the street would join me and we would skate to Seward Park, where we could show off with our new forward glides and our backward hip-hippety movement. There we would meet girls of other streets and we would race them around the square or hitch on to wagons just to parade the daring of our Street.

Near midnight, I would skate home and sit on the stoop with my mother and the other men and women of the house.

There would be a thrumming and a tingling in my feet and I would feel as if I were still skating.

On the evenings that there was dancing on the roof of the public school on Houston Street, Lena, who had fuzzy hair and danced beautifully, would call for me and we would go there.

The roof was all lit up, and a regular orchestra with a fiddle played for us. There were hundreds of girls all dressed up and clean, all partnered off. In the middle, with the whistle in her mouth, stood the playground teacher. Around her, we danced.

Sometimes she selected one truly fortunate and danced with her at the head of the line. That event never occurred to me, although I wished for it with all my heart.

We danced the minuet, the sword dance, and folk dances, all of which we had learned at school. Sometimes we danced the ribbon dance using paper ribbons, and that would color the entire week for me. It was a complicated thing and required three people, not just two.

Once on returning from a roof dance, Lena and I walked down my street feeling very happy and most unearthly.

We hummed and were silent and then hummed again.

We sat down on my stoop, silent and awed by the happiness of the evening.

Suddenly we heard a groan from a house on the opposite side of the street. We looked up. It came from a fire escape on the second floor. There was bedding spread on it and a girl's face was pressed against the bars. Her hair fell on each side of her face in wet steaks.

"Who's that?" I whispered, as if the girl could overhear us.

"That's Millie Kessel," Lena replied. "She just came home from the hospital."

"What's the matter with her?"

"Her foot is poisoned. Every day they have to cut out a piece away from it," Lena explained with a certain relish. "But now they can't cut any more. She's poisoned all over. My mother says it's because she washed her feet in cold water and then went out into the cold with summer underwear on. She's fourteen going on fifteen."

That night, I awoke. It seemed to me that I heard Millie Kessel groaning.

The next morning my mother's eyes were red. Millie Kessel had died in the night.

"Promise me you won't come to the hall," my mother begged.

My mother was going to be married to the boarder, Noosan. The wedding was to take place that evening in the hall on the opposite side of the street. My mother seemed very frightened and she made me go with her into the bedroom where she picked me up like a baby and sat me on the splendidly ornate bed—heaped high with feather beds and covered with a cheap lace set. I protested and squirmed down. I wasn't a baby! What was the matter with her?

"Promise me you won't come," my mother repeated. Her strained manner communicated itself to me. I could not take my eyes off her, try as I did. She stood out to me in a black, intangible frame that shut out everything else. She talked in a curiously low tone. I was surprised. I felt that this was not my mother but some stranger.

"It isn't right for a child to go to her own mother's wedding," she said. She wiped the corners of her mouth with her thumb and forefinger and drew her lips together despairingly.

"You mean I should go away?" I asked.

"Yeh." My mother nodded and then added quickly, "Here's fifteen cents for a pair of new silk stockings. And here is ten cents more. You can take Margaret Leizer to the nickel show."

I took the money. A look of cunning must have spread over my face, for my mother drew me quickly to her.

"But you understand you mustn't come to the hall. You must stay away from the wedding. Now, promise me, Honeyle."

I promised. Pushing my mother away from me with both hands, I ran out of the house. I did not stop until I reached Margaret's store on the next block.

"Wanna come with me and buy silk stockin's?" I asked.

Margaret shook her head. "Can't. I got to mind the store. Come on in."

I went in and stayed for a while, eating coffee beans from an open, sun-heated sack. I didn't really eat them. I chewed them, stuck my head through the open door, and spat them out into the street in rhythmic motion.

I felt oppressed. I felt as if my mother had tricked me into something dishonorable, not so much by her marriage as by her feverish desire to keep me out of the hall.

"Feel sick?" Margaret asked. She sat on a swivel stool which creaked maddeningly.

"No."

"Sorry your momma's getting married?"

"No," I replied heavily, "I don't care one bit."

I rose and spat the last coffee bean out of my mouth, unchewed.

"Where yuh gawn?" Margaret asked.

"Buy the stockin's."

"Let's spend the money on ice cream and candy," Margaret suggested.

"No," I replied doggedly. "My mother said I should buy stockin's."

To my mind, the purchase of the stockings was as much a part of my mother's wedding as the marriage canopy.

There was a peculiar singing in my head as I walked up to Willet* and Rivington Streets where I bought my stockings. Gradually it resolved itself into a tune to which I set my own words. In that way, I pitied myself.

I bargained with the peddler, an old woman with no teeth. She finally let me have the stockings—damaged at the toe and the top—swearing that she didn't make a cent on the transaction.

Usually I would have taken keen pride in scoring such a bargain, but now I didn't. The events of the day, including the purchase of the stockings, had acquired a curious unreality for me. I wasn't sure whether it was I who was walking up Rivington Street or someone else.

I walked to Clinton Street and then turned back to meet Margaret.

She was already at the entrance to the movies.

We spent two hours looking at the screen and then came out to find the streets dark and the lights on. I couldn't go home yet.

---

*What remains of Willet Street has been renamed Bialystocker Place . —*R.L.*

It was only a little past nine. And I still had two cents.

"I got two cents," I told Margaret.

"Let's get two glasses of soda water," Margaret suggested. "I know a place far up where you can get a lot."

Finding the stand, getting our soda water, looking in store windows, and getting back destroyed an hour for me. Then it was only quarter past ten.

"I'm going home," announced Margaret.

"Don't go, it's early," I begged. I was afraid to be left alone.

"Early! It's late," Margaret declared. "I'll tell you what, I'll walk you to your house and then I'll go home."

I squeezed Margaret's hand for thanks. Leisurely, we walked to the front of the stoop of the house in which I lived. From the hall across the street, the hectic, boisterous sounds of a Hungarian *czardas* reached me. There was a flute, a violin, and a cornet.

"Come up, I'll see if the door's open," I cried, taking hold of Margaret's wayward hand. Margaret had heard the music, too.

But the door was locked.

"What'll you do?" Margaret asked me curiously.

"Nothing." The tears were close to my eyes.

Margaret leaned over to me. "I dare you go to your mother's wedding," she whispered.

The boldness of her "dare" took my voice away for a moment. "Oh, but I can't," I assured her earnestly.

"I dare you," repeated Margaret wickedly. "Say you want to get the key to the apartment."

That was legitimate.

"But you gotta come with me," I said.

Margaret promised and we clattered down the stairs. On the stoop, people looked at me curiously and exchanged thin smiles.

Margaret held tight to my hand and before I was aware of it I found myself looking at my stepfather. My mother was dancing.

He wore a new black suit and a black derby. He was working his mouth—he may have been finishing his supper—and his hat rose and fell with each move of his head. Fascinated, I watched that sustained motion.*

My mother seemed very gay and was executing one of the fancy steps that the czardas numbers.

No one appeared to see me and then everybody at once seemed to be surrounding me. I could see my mother in her old-rose silk dress looking at me, eyes struggling with anger. Other eyes seemed amused. The music had stopped and the musicians rose to look at me. My stepfather alone kept his seat.

"I told you, you shouldn't come," my mother said, her voice thick with feeling.

"I came for the key, the door is locked."

I looked around for Margaret to substantiate for me, but she had disappeared.

Some of the men set up a roaring laugh and the women joined.

"Let her stay here," one woman begged.

"Sure, let her say that she danced on her mother's wedding. Not many daughters can say that," amended a man, and the wedding guests laughed afresh—my mother among them.

I remained. I danced and danced, with or without partners. I danced to the last lingering note of the flute.

The next morning, I was conscious only of having lost my silk stockings—the silk stockings I had gotten for twelve cents.

Life in our home continued in the same tumultuous uneventfulness. My mother sewed for others and waited upon her boarders just as she had before her marriage.

I regarded my stepfather with the same indifference I had felt for him when he was our boarder, Noosan.

One night, as I was taking up my skates after supper, he

---

*The wearing of a hat indoors, where "American" men would be hatless, suggests that Noosan was an observant Jew, at least on the occasion of his marriage. Bella and her mother's formal attachment to their religion is evident only at the end of the memoir, on another ceremonial occasion. —R.L.

summoned me to him. "You'd better call me father."

I shook my head and smiled.

My mother stood and looked at us anxiously.

"No," I answered.

My stepfather flushed angrily. "You hear that, Fanny?" he said.

"Give her time to get used to you," my mother placated.

"Not even in a hundred years. Or a thousand," I cried and rushed out of the house.

The settlement on Madison Street now gripped me.* On Saturday afternoons there was club, and on certain afternoons and evenings, there were rehearsals for the play we were going to give.

The club, composed of a dozen girls who went to school with me, was led by Mrs. Slazens, a kind, maternal woman who came from uptown and spoke with a slight lisp. She was my idea of an ideal mother.

Our play was a humorous one and dealt with a village of old maids all of whom were in love with one man. The only girl with a husky voice was chosen for the male lead, and the rest of us played the spinster roles or acted as stage hands and dresser.

I forgot home, mother, and stepfather in the strenuous days that emerged for me as producer and leading lady.

The play ran for three nights! It was the great success of the settlement house. We gave it for friends and supporters of the house who came from uptown. We gave it for the other clubs of the house. And we gave it for an audience of mothers who understood little of what was going on but laughed as heartily as those from uptown.

Following our theatrical success, Mrs. Slazens invited the

---

*Formally Madison House of the Downtown Ethical Society, the settlement house stood at 216 Madison Street. In the 1950s it merged with another settlement, Hamilton House, and is now located at 50 Madison Street, where it serves a largely Asian clientele. More so in Bella's time than in ours, when the concept of the "melting pot" has been exchanged for multiculturalism, the settlement house movement served, with the schools, to Americanize immigrants. Bella's piano lessons were also courtesy of Madison House. —R.L.

club to her home.

It was the day of days for us. Going as far uptown as Ninety-sixth Street would have made it special even without the invitation. Not one of us had ever been as far as that.

Only three of us had hats. The rest of us bought or borrowed.

We rode up in the subway as a group, trying hard not to laugh and not to call out to each other.

"Do you think we'll have cake and ice cream?" Clara Mill asked. She liked food.

Gussie, who was more of a lady than any one of us, stared at her frozenly.

"I'm only asking," Clara weakly apologized.

The house had an elevator! The house had a marble hall! And a man opened the outside door for you!

We could only look at one another with wide eyes.

Such magnificence! Such opulence!

A maid in a little white apron and cap opened the door for us. But Mrs. Slazens herself welcomed us all into the apartment. And she wore a lovely silk dress with a white lace collar. Behind her, hanging back shyly, stood a little girl of eight.

This was Tess, Mrs. Slazen's baby.

We regarded her as curiously as she regarded us and then filed into the living room and seated ourselves stiffly.

Mrs. Slazen excused herself and tactfully left us alone. We hopped up from our chairs and snooped about the room. We looked at the books, the pictures, the music, the piano, the flow-ers—everything!

By the time Mrs. Slazens returned with the maid bearing ice cream and cake, we were thoroughly at home. So much so that Clara Mill, about to get a second helping of the ice cream, called out to Gussie, "I told you, Gus, we'd get ice cream and cake!"

Gussie played the piano and we sang. Mrs. Slazens sang too.

Riding back to the Lower East Side, we called out to each other and shouted and laughed. We didn't have to be ladies now. We were riding down—not up!

Several months later, a thin little gray-haired woman with the smallest, shiniest shoes I had ever seen came to visit the club. She announced that the settlement was going to give a play called "The Dryad and the Kiss" and that those wishing to take part should come to her after the meeting.

And I was chosen for the part of the Dryad!

But I never played it, for on the night of its presentation my mother gave birth to my brother Herschey.

My stepfather came to look at his son frequently as he lay in a niche beside my mother.

"He looks like *my* side," he told himself and touched the moist, soft-boned little hand with his blunt fingers. Some of the girls and men who owed my mother money brought the little fellow gifts of knitted baby sets and silk coats trimmed with wide lace. When my mother slept, I would lift the splendid little things from their pasteboard boxes and pat them gently.

The cradle—of yellow wood—arrived on a Saturday. My mother lifted the straw-filled little mattress and my stepfather scattered three cents worth of jelly beans over the spring. My mother had insisted on this to ensure the baby worldly success.

On top of the hard little mattress my mother placed a pillow. At the head of the cradle, she carefully patted into comfortable positions two diminutive pillows, whose edges were stiff with needlework. I lowered the baby into his cradle. His bright flitting eyes stared at us interestedly.

I touched the cradle lightly and it swayed for a moment and then stood still.

"He smiled," my mother cried. "He smiled."

"Ah—what are you talking about? He's too young," my stepfather scoffed.

"I am too happy. Things are going too well for me," my mother said to me. She was nursing the baby, who looked up inquiringly from her breast. He was now six months old. My mother already talked about the future appearance of his teeth.

"Look how contented we are here. We have our bread and meat and milk. The house is clean and Noosan is prospering. He has sent for his brother to come here from Europe, and he sends money to his people almost every week. Yesterday I paid the last installment on the sideboard and the icebox. The table I paid cash for, you remember. Now, you tell me, my brave youngster, is there anything we have to complain of?"

My brother, to whom my mother had addressed her last remark, stretched out his twittering little rose-tipped fingers to her lips and then turned back savagely to her breast.

"True, I should like to stop sewing and keeping boarders. When a woman has so many boarders, it makes her feel as if she were going after dirty pigs in her own home. But Noosan says he doesn't always want to be a worker. And can you blame him?"

My mother looked at me sharply. "I've been talking all this time, and not so much as a peep have I heard from you," she demanded playfully. Her eyes softened. "You're happy too, aren't you, Honeyle?"

My mother's attention was distracted from me by the soft insistent patting hands of my brother.

"Who is my equal?" my mother asked softly, her eyes full of love and gratitude. "Who, so fortunate as I?"

The next night, my mother woke me up and asked me to look at Herschey's face. A curious red sore had appeared on his pink cheek and there were signs of others coming up.

"It's nothing," I told her, "nothing—it'll pass away."

"You think so?" My mother, I could see, hung desperately on what I was saying.

I did think so. Our next-door neighbor was called in during the day, and she shrugged her shoulders and called my mother a fool for being worried.

My mother took the baby to the doctor and returned with a black salve. Herschey's little face was smeared with it, but the sore festered and the child fretted. My stepfather looked at the child, squirming and yelping with pain, and I saw his face harden.

77

"Did the doctor say he'd be all right?" he asked my mother tensely.

"Yes—yes—he said it'll go away," she assured him, kneeling at the side of the crib and stroking the child's hands. They were still clear.

The following day, the baby's hands and arms were covered, but the sores did not spread to his beautifully formed body. I was thankful for that.

As the hopelessness of ever driving this painful disfigurement away was borne in upon us, our house changed. It became slovenly and looked dark even when the sun shone. My stepfather said less than he had ever said before. Whenever he did speak to my mother, it was to jeer at her. He stepped forward as a bitter man who felt himself to have been wronged by my mother. Night after night, after everyone had gone to bed, he would lash her with his tongue. He accused her of having duped him into marriage. At first, my mother tried to conciliate him and fabricated reasons for his manner. As it continued, she grew silent. One night she came out of her silence, and then the two debated until the stars left the sky.

My stepfather began by sighing heavily. And then as if the sighs cleared his throat, he started off for the night. "But I tell you it's impossible for me to live with you."

After a silence, which my mother did not break, he continued self-pityingly. "When I married you, you knew that we were not suited. We were no pair. You nagged me until I was a laughing-stock in the eyes of all my friends. I and you!" My stepfather laughed shortly in a shrill soprano and flung the covers about. "You had a great deal of boldness to make me marry you. You! A woman with a child. Why— why—I could have married a young girl with money. And to think how you tricked me. *Gotteinu!*"*

---

*Probably assuming that her readers would not be familiar with Yiddish expressions, Bella wrote "God mine"—neither Yiddish nor English. —*R.L.*

Both my mother and I lay with our eyes wide open, my mother's tears running down her face. I listened indifferently, trying hard to get a little sleep in the pauses that came now and then.

My mother spoke now in a dry, hard monotone that contrasted strangely with her wet face. "Did I fool you into marrying me? Ask yourself that question. You know better. You know that I could now be living with a servant in the house instead of wiping up the spit of men who would not have dared to talk to me in the old country. Their mothers would come to us for a piece of bread—"

A kicking laugh from the other side of the room, where my stepfather lay, brought more tears. For a while, I dropped off to sleep but was awakened by my mother's deadened voice. "As for my child, I never hid her or told you that she wasn't mine. Why do you scoff at her? I bore her virtuously."

My mother's self-control left her and she stopped, lest she cry out loud.

"How do I know that?" my stepfather cried.

I felt my mother's body grow rigid. I placed my hand over her mouth. I was now awake.

"How do I know you were decent?" he continued. "By your countrymen? They are no better than you are." And then suddenly, as if unable to stand his own equable manner of stating things, he beat his head upon the wall, crying, "You wretch! You have brought me trouble! You have borne me a sickly child. And a son, God in heaven, a son!" He sobbed aloud.

My mother replied, "Have I not been a good wife to you? Have I not kept the house without your help? Do you forget that I am still sewing? That I sewed to the last minute? That when I told you I was tired, you said I would be more tired of having nothing to do if I stopped. Nothing to do! I don't throw it up to you, Noosan, but is it just for you to eat me with your words? What woman would do for you all I have done? What woman pays the rent of a house? Am I ugly that you should want to leave me?"

Her placating voice roused my stepfather to full fury. He

stood up in the bed and wept at the top of his voice. "Oh, what have you done to my son?"

By the time the summer dragged itself almost to a close, I was a full-fledged "little mother." I fed, cleaned, and dressed the baby. I was with him all day and nearly all night. My baby brother slept in his carriage on the street while I watched, and in the house, my mother worked feverishly at her sewing.

I would stay on the street until two in the morning, my head pillowed in my lap.

I went to the settlement only on rare occasions. The backdrop was changing for me.

In the house, I would catch my stepfather's eyes fixed on me with a curious, jeering stare. I avoided him as much as I could.

A month later my mother came to the corner where I was taking care of my brother in his carriage. She had been crying. "Noosan is going to leave me," she said. Her face worked piteously.

"But how do you know?"

"I know," my mother said sadly.

"Why don't you arrest him?" I seemed to know how to handle the situation better than my mother. It was because she had leaned on me for so long a time, I suppose.

"I can't arrest him," she muttered. "I can't."

"Why?" I was impatient. "Hasn't he done enough to you already?"

"But he is still my husband."

"Then hang yourself with him," I said shortly.

In the morning, my stepfather left us with the jauntiest smile he had ever worn. He got up considerably earlier than usual because, as he said, he had damaged a pair of pants at the shop and wanted to get the stain out before his foreman arrived.

That smile and his swinging gait—

We never saw him again.

PART IV

Goerck Street

Goerck Street is one block below Lewis and two blocks from the East River.* Every move we made brought us closer to it. Our street began with a saloon on Houston Street. Next to it stood a lumberyard whose entrance every Sunday morning was marked by a garbage heap to which all contributed. Then came our row of houses. On the Stanton Street corner was another saloon.

I went several times to Goerck Street before we moved, compelled by fear and dread. It was a "tough" block. From there would come every offensive in the bottle fights that would visit Lewis, Cannon, Columbia, and Sheriff streets like some short, noisy pestilence. Bottle fights included every kind of weapon; some of the Goerck Street gangs used to throw rusty blades.

As a very little girl I would dare myself at night to go to Goerck Street and never get any further than the corner. Ours was and still is one of a row of red four-story houses, a fifth story

---

*Goerck Street disappeared when, in another effort at slum clearance, the Corlears Hook and Baruch Houses were erected. —*R.L.*

being based on the stoop. There was a constant going and coming of moving vans and pushcarts—one family moved into one house and another moved out of the next. The houses formed a drably indifferent village that on rainy days looked like a row of washed-out, badly patched petticoats. They shared their submerging sorrows, small sufficient joys, and frequent fights. The majority of the families sprang from Galician sources; the rest were Hungarian and German Jews and a few Russians. The first half of the next block was Jewish and the rest of it was Italian, with an invisible but definite line of demarcation.

Our house, like the others, had four families on each floor, two to the rear and two to the front. There were two windows to the front room which either faced the street or the yard, one window in the kitchen that faced an exceedingly narrow, lightless airshaft, and in the bedroom a tiny square window that faced the hall. The hall had no window at all on any floor and got its heat and ventilation from the street. This is true of most East Side tenements. Separating the front room from the kitchen is what my mother called a "blind" window. It was simply a square hole, framed by woodwork, which allowed some of the front light to filter into the kitchen and stop at the entrance to the bedroom.

From the East River, night and day, came the hooting of ferryboats and transient ships.

On this street the chains tightened.

We were moved from Lewis to Goerck Street by a pushcart because that was cheapest. It took several trips to move us. We spent the day getting the rooms to look homelike—that is, a place to eat, work, and sleep, eat, work, and sleep. In the front room: the icebox, sideboard, table, chairs, and bed. In the kitchen: stove, table, and foldingbed. In the bedroom, another bed. Home!

"The woman who lived here left us a legacy," my mother remarked facetiously. "We'll have a hard time getting rid of these roaches."

I was standing in the front room, now containing our bed, Herschey's cradle and carriage, a not altogether qualifying mirror, three chairs, a round dining-room table, the sideboard, and the icebox. "What does it matter?" I looked through the window. In one apartment across the street, I saw a girl combing her long brown hair, her uncovered arms rising and falling like chords being struck on a harp. In another apartment, I saw a little boy clinging to his mother's hips, his face turned up prayerfully to her. He was probably asking for a penny. In still another, a man was raising his fist to strike.

I could see things quite clearly. The cobblestoned street was very narrow.

My mother continued her examinations. "There's a rat hole here as big as my hand," she said. "We'll put some tin over it tomorrow, I'm too tired now."

She came into the room where I was standing and seated herself wearily upon the bed.

"Be careful, Herschey's there," I cautioned.

"And I didn't even know." She smiled wanly. "It will soon be night. Again going to sleep and again getting up." My mother sighed. She stirred herself as if to rise. "I better make you some coffee."

"I'll do it myself," I said. My voice sounded harsh—like heel-crunched gravel. "When will this all end? . . . God, if there is a God, when will it end?" Like drumsticks, rat-tat-tatting on a drum, these questions beat on my tired consciousness until I fell asleep.

At midnight, I opened my eyes with an effort. There, on the window ledge, sat three rats, as large as week-old kittens, regarding us in the bed with excited squeaks.

I picked up a shoe and threw it at them. The rats cried excitedly and I could hear them scurrying down their hole, squeaking in fear and amazement.

One snow-draped day, not long after we moved, I was graduated with several hundred others from my public school. During the exercises, bits of Bible text which our principal had read to us at the opening of each school day kept going through my head just as the flakes outside fell before my eyes.

"Make a joyful noise into the Lord. . . . Praise the earth with gladness. . . . And there was light. . . . The wages of sin is death. . . . Vengeance is mine, saith the Lord. . . . When a man smite thee. . . . For the thing which I greatly feared is come upon me. . . . The heavens declare the glory of God. . . ."

When the exercises were over and the sound of the school orchestra had lost its insistent sharpness, a great peace descended on me. I remembered the preaching voices of the elders who had talked to us only as I would have remembered them in a dream. Even the teachers I had had during my school years crowded themselves into tinier shelves of the backroom consciousness, including those who had hurt me grievously and those who had gladdened me with words of praise or understanding.

In the wet playground waited "a sister-graduate"—Celia. She was Russian, the fourth child of seven. I began to like Celia when she appeared in a new red flannel dress to take her oath of office in our system of school government. She had pranced up to the platform in the auditorium looking like some queer, long-legged bird—her blond hair, the color of an uncleaned brass faucet, standing up and around her thin, pointed face; her large round glasses catching the reflected lights of the afternoon sun; her wide pale mouth parted to show bits of greenish patchwork teeth.

Celia and I walked home together in meditating silence. We looked very grave as we ascended the stairs to the fifth floor where Celia lived, for I was to try to persuade her mother and father to let her go to high school. I was not sure of myself but I wouldn't give up the fight as easily as Celia had. I found the house in the usual state of disorder. Moishey, the youngest, was very anxious to go out on the fire escape because it was snowing and his mother was loudly assuring him that he would catch cold and die if he did.

"Let it be with luck." She turned from her youngest to greet me in her musical Russian-Jewish dialect.

"It will have to be," I said a bit arrogantly in my broader, sharper Hungarian Yiddish.

"You are going to high school?" she asked me curiously. Celia's mother was a large woman with a very small head bristling with iron-gray curly ends.

"Yes," I answered quickly, although I was not sure, "and I have come to ask you why you won't let Celia go." The woman's eyes opened a bit. I had raised my voice.

"Yes," I continued, my voice getting a sharp edge to it, "why shouldn't you let Celia go to high school? She's got more than I, and my mother's letting me."

"But you don't understand," Celia's mother assured me. "You are a child. Every little money that comes into the house counts. Celia must go working. We know it's hard, but what can we do? There are three more that must go through public school, no? Three more need shoes and shirts and dresses and food. There isn't enough. My husband makes but very little. He is no more a young one. Wouldn't we let Celia go if we could? Of course! Don't talk foolish!"

Celia's mother regarded me with mildly reproving eyes. A child of thirteen trying to teach her something—!

But I continued. I was there to fight for Celia's chance. Celia herself sat in the very cold front room. She was too full of tears to trust herself to help me in her cause. Hadn't she talked until the spit came out at the corners of her mouth? Hadn't she got herself whipped for the things she had already said to her father on the matter? Oh, what was the use!

"But you don't understand—" I broke out exasperated— "Celia is the smartest girl in the school. She is an orator! She is a leader! All she needs is high school. What'll you get out of her if you send her to a factory or an office? You know how much. Three dollars a week, maybe four! Maybe at the end of the four years, she'll make ten dollars a week. I know it's a lot, ten dollars, but if you let her go to high school, at the end of the four years she can be a playground teacher—a big woman! She can make fifteen dollars a week right off. After school she can work and make a little money for the house. You must let her go to high school. She mustn't become a factory girl!"

Celia's mother shrugged her shoulders patiently. "Me, it doesn't trouble. She can go for my part. Talk to her father."

At this moment, her father, who had been asleep, emerged from the bedroom, tugging at his suspenders. "Hah? What is this about?"

He was a big, broad-boned man with a slight cast in his left eye. I regarded him speculatively. How did one tackle fathers?

I repeated my arguments to him in a small voice.

"It cannot be. Celia must go to work," he said at the end of my speech, with a finality that knew no dispute. "You're only a little girl. You don't understand."

"I don't understand?" I repeated, in what was supposed to be sarcasm, "I don't understand? Do you know that I have no father and that my mother is sending me just the same? Celia *has* a father."

The proof of my assertion hitched up his suspenders again and turned to his wife. "The supper is made?" he asked. I was dismissed. Celia accompanied me into the hall and down into the street.

"It's no use." The tears were beginning to fall down her gray, thin cheeks. "It's no use."

Two days later, Celia entered a sweater factory.

The opposition at Celia's house strengthened me in my resolve to get to high school and through it, whatever happened.

And my mother was with me because it meant that I would be a lady.

Several days later I tripped up the steps of the Washington Irving High School, missed my footing, thought of William the Conquerer and mechanically added "1066 A.D." My hand held tightly the transfer card from the Hunter College High School, which I had been attending in a state of misery. I had asked for the transfer because the carfares were a drain on our poverty.*

Within the splendid but still unfinished foyer, I felt strangely elated. The transfer must have excited me.

I heard several workmen hammering away in some distant part of the building.

"I am the God Thor, I am the God of War," I felt moved to say under my breath. I wondered whether if I shouted I would hear my echo. I essayed a faint round noise and then hastily clapped my hand over my mouth.

I was now skipping from one door to the other reading the numbers. The strange elation had not left me. I was to find the Latin room. I opened its door, closed it behind me, and looked at a tall, pliant, narrow-boned woman standing at the board, her face toward me. The room receded and all I saw was the Latin

---

*There are two ways to interpret this information: (1) that she hated Hunter College High School and used the carfare—ten cents for the round trip to Sixty-eighth Street and Lexington Avenue—as an excuse to transfer out, or (2) that having to spend fifty cents a week, a full half of the money she was able to earn for one day's work in the sweatshop, made her miserable.

Certainly the carfare would have been a heavy burden, particularly as she was able to walk to Washington Irving High School, less than two miles from her home. Yet given Bella's intellectual avidity, Hunter High should have been her school of choice, it being the most rigorous of the public high schools for females. In which case, she would have viewed the carfare as a fair trade-off, as presumably she did when she enrolled.

On the other hand, her misery may have resulted more directly from the "tone" of Hunter High School, where the students in that period, mostly from families of a higher social class than her own, were required to behave in a seriously ladylike manner. A spirit as free and determined as Bella's may well have felt friendless and constrained at Hunter High, where academic excellence was only one of the demands made on its students. —R.L.

teacher. Her hair was a clean, soft brown and was plaited twice around her head. I could not take my eyes off her. I had never seen such virile beauty before. It made my throat dry. I thought of the Stone profile.

A whisper kept going through the class. It grew louder and louder. It seemed to be directed at me. I faced the girls, but the teacher's face blurred them all together. Gradually, their faces became individually distinct and I cried out with joy, for among them I recognized girls with whom I had gone to grade school.

"Hello!" I called out and then we all began to laugh.

And the teacher laughed too!

After we had gotten ourselves settled in our new home, Mother began to sew feverishly, night and day. She even tried to earn money by bringing about a match between a girl who was thirty-two, short-waisted and budding with a moustache, and a man whose right leg was a little shorter than his left. The two could not reconcile themselves to each other's shortcomings, however, and my mother found herself the loser by much time and the girl's friendship. Another girl who worked in a ladies' neckwear factory and who had a skirt made at my mother's wanted to get married very badly. I quote my mother: "Eating, lying down, waking up, she wanted to get married." But my mother could find no one for her.

I always think with pity of this girl—she was like a skeleton, her sallow cheeks drawn and thin and badly rouged. She measured four feet. Yet she wished to marry and give children to the earth. To conceal her thinness, she would have her skirts pleated and wore the Merry Widow collars then in vogue whose steels reached almost above her ears. Once she came to show us a new hat she had bought. It was a large one, with a whole garden on it as my mother put it. It was on the occasion of this hat that she confided to me that in her shop a man had once been in love with her.

"Every step I took, his eyes followed me," she said, looking into my eyes with her own lovesick ones, "but he left the shop one day, and I—I have never seen him again from that day on."

"Did you give him any money?" I asked brutally.

"Money?" What are you talking about?" The little figure drew itself up haughtily. "A man would have to be made of gold for me to give him money!"

Yet I could see in her very manner that she was lying. I was sorry for having attempted to prick her self-constructed bubble.

"I was just making fun," I amended lamely.

"That's all right," she simpered forgivingly and pulled the points of her collar up closer to her ears.

About this time, I went to work on Sundays in a man's coat shop on our street near the corner. The shop was on the top floor of a tall loft building next to the lumberyard.

The young, stoutish boss knew that I was going to high school because several landsleit of my mother's worked in that shop and his manner was one of mixed deference and defiance toward his soon-to-be-a-lady worker. He showed me what my work would be as a trimmer, and I followed his directions. I had brought with me a pair of shears and needle. All I did was cut off the various pieces of alpaca and buckram which the operator had left when seaming together the sleeves or parts of the coat. These I dropped into a large laundry basket at my feet.

The monotony of the work was soothing and restful—the thrum of the machines and the pounding of the heavy flatirons a lullaby. Now and then I caught a pair of eyes fixed on me in curious wonder. They belonged to a young, red-cheeked operator whom I did not know. He must have been nineteen or twenty. I looked at him inquiringly and smiled. He bent over his work at the machine, but the smile had spread over his face.

At the noon break, an old, gray-bearded peddler stomped into the shop with a cheery remark on the length of the stairs and the short windedness of his breath. He brought some seltzer and several siphons, a basket of fruit, and cheap unwrapped candy.

The operator looked at me with a hopeful smile trembling at his still unmustached lips. I looked back at him in doubt. What did he want?

Then as if with a sudden resolve he left his chair and advanced to the peddler.

"Here, old man, give this Fräulein a good glass of water," he ordered in a loud blustering tone.

But I didn't want any, I told him. The operator looked like an empty paper bag which, after it has been filled with air to its very corners, is suddenly banged against a wall. The old peddler looked at me pleadingly. For him, it meant a sale. I took the glass of water and drank every bit of it. I was thirsty.

"And a piece of chungum?" the peddler suggested craftily, holding up a stick of chewing gum.

The operator put his hand into his pocket as if to pay for it—if only I would accept.

This time I shook my head vehemently. I did not want chewing gum.

I retreated into my corner, for I had no wish to go down into the street. The stairs were so long and to come up again—no. The operator sat tipped back on his chair and looked at me.

After a half hour the whistle blew again and the shop resumed its thrumming and pounding. At the end of the day, six o'clock for me, I said good-night to the boss and said I would report next Sunday.

When I came home, I found my mother in pain and Herschey unfed. I was kept busy until eight, helping her to bed and feeding and cleaning my little brother. Then I washed a few little dresses, torn and discolored from frequent wear, and hung them on the fire escape, for there was no clothesline in the back.

When I came home from school the next day, my mother told me that my boss had come and paid a dollar for my services, but he didn't want me to come any more. I felt as if I had been slapped.

"But why?" I demanded. "I worked hard."

"He said he doesn't want you in the shop," my mother repeated with a faint smile. The smile deepened.

"He said that I should treat you well, should fatten you out a little," my mother added, now laughing aloud. "He says he wants to marry you."

"Marry!"

My mother nodded, wiping the tears of mirth from her eyes. "But I told him all right. I told him Fanny's Honeyle would be a Lady!"

My mother was not often gay now. When she wasn't going to "Twenty-first Street," as the United Hebrew Charities were called by those who had to ask organized charity's aid, she was at home working feverishly on somebody else's baby dresses, pillowcases, sheets, skirts, and dresses.

Each time she would return, her flushed face and feverish eyes would tell me the answer. There was nothing. Once she came back and cried bitterly upon the bed—she had cried just that way when my stepfather abandoned her. Mrs. Schlisselfeld, the neighbor in the rear, a sentimental, large-nosed woman with enough troubles of her own to have made her a cynic, came in on hearing my mother cry. Her only son, a boy of seven or eight, was an idiot—a healthy, full-grown, stuttering idiot.

To her, my mother told the story. She had gone to Twenty-first Street to tell them that any moment she would have a child and that they should pity her and pay her rent for her. "It is so hard for me to work. Only those who wish me evil should feel my pains," my mother wailed.

When she had got there, the rain was coming down in sheets. My little brother Herschey was on her arm. Mr. H., an assistant and therefore a dignitary in his own right, came over to my mother and took her by the fat of her free arm.

"Such a woman like you—" he said, squeezing her arm, "shouldn't come here for help."

He looked directly into her eyes. My mother, without even thinking of the consequences, struck out and hit him directly on the mouth. Misery is a good propelling force.

Mr. H. cried out for aid, but the sergeant-at-arms, who was stationed there to eject such poor as were not wanted, was not on the scene.

"Get out of here this minute!" cried Mr. H. "Get out. Don't you dare show your face in here again. You will not get a penny from us!"

He backed my mother out into the rain, my sick little brother in her arms.

All this my mother cried out to Mrs. Schlisselfeld. And Mrs. Schlisselfeld cried with her.

When my mother first went to Twenty-first Street, she told us she joined the men, women, and children in the basement. There, they were subjected to a series of questions. No matter how old the poor were, the questions were just as ferreting. Sensitiveness displayed by the applicant in showing how far sunken he was, was like a red rag to the bull—the questioner.

As my mother waited for her turn at the desk, she could not help but pity a Russian woman who was beating her head with her fists and crying fiercely. She was dressed in cast-off clothes of the worst type. She was recommended by the desk to have her rent paid—sixteen dollars.

My mother was so overcome with pity for this woman that she could not help following her with her eyes as she went up the stairs.

"I was looking like this," my mother told us, "when I saw the well-pressed little ruffles of her petticoat and the silk stocking underneath her rags. I didn't make any ruckus, not like she had. I just told what had happened to me and how I needed help, but I didn't get it. To get help from that place, burned it should only be, you must cry and tear your hair and eat the dirt on the floor. Then they believe you."

While my mother was drawn down to the floor by the pain she felt more and more frequently, the investigator of the charity happened in. She was about twenty, red-haired and white-toothed. She wore a broad hat. I remember her. As she saw my mother lying on the floor, the cold sweat of fear on her face, the investigator said, "Why do you act for me? It won't help you. No amount of acting will."

My mother ignored her and kept crying out to Mrs. Schlisselfeld, the kind neighbor in the rear, who came running in to see whether this time the baby had really arrived.

She was in time to hear this investigator finish her lecture to my mother on the floor—on not to act—not to pretend; it doesn't help.

Mrs. Schlisselfeld was a gentle soul and so she interposed quietly. "Don't you see that this woman is going to have a baby?"

She didn't know that, the investigator acknowledged in stiff confusion. It is strange that she didn't, for my mother's record must have been known to her from the moment my stepfather had left her. And if not, then what were her green, ferreting eyes for? To detect pots boiling on the stove? To see whether there were any men in the house? To notice whether the house was too clean to indicate poverty?

Another investigator whom I remember was a tall fat woman of about thirty-five. She was a majestic creature with a look of hauteur on her face that as much invited confidence as the smirk on the face of a cat that invites the mouse out of its hole.

Mrs. Schlisselfeld, feeling sure that my mother was going to give birth to a child, sent me for Dr. Grossman. My mother lay in the bed moaning and crying, her head rolling from side to side.

"Oh, my feet are like glass. My feet are like glass. . . . He was afraid that the second would be like the first and so he left me. Sweet child, never leave me. . . . Oh, my feet are like glass. God, my God, what are you doing to me?"

The doctor arrived, ordered the blinds pulled down, himself closed the shutters and lit the two gas jets. The room became unbearably hot and Herschey began to cry.

I took him and went down into the street.

A small group had collected on the opposite side and were pointing at the windows of our rooms. They were talking about us . . . about the charity . . . about how my stepfather had run away from my mother.

Fiercely I clasped Herschey to me and rocked him in my arms. I sang to him strange, wild words for, although I was no longer a child, the habit of my early childhood returned to me. I composed weird tunes to rid myself of the feelings that seemed to burst my neck open. I raised my clenched fist against those hurtfully curious people on the other side of the street.

Gradually, Herschey fell asleep, one of his tiny sore-ridden hands reaching up to my throat. I placed him in his carriage—the carriage that had been brought home for the first time so tri-umphantly—and seated myself on the stoop near him. My mother's shrieks of pain cut through the shut windows. I lowered my head into my lap and tried to sleep.

As the hours slowly dragged by and the street grew quieter, I began to drowse a bit.

"Get up, come upstairs."

I felt a hand that smelled moistly of salt and tomatoes. I took Herschey into my arms and laid him into his cradle where he curled up again and continued to sleep. Then I dragged his perambulator upstairs, not feeling the annoyance I usually felt when it bumped up noisily.

I stood in the kitchen and stared vacantly at the soiled dish-es on the washtub. The doctor came in. His glasses were filmed. His short, fat body caved in with weariness. Mrs. Schlisselfeld sidled up to him in the manner of a whipped dog to his master. She addressed him as "Sir Doctor."

They talked in whispers while my mother moaned softly, as

if to assure herself that she was still alive.

"We need another doctor." The man turned to me suddenly. "Run out and get one, any one!"

I hurried into the deserted street and ran in and out—in and out to Fourth Street—Doctor Row. It was past midnight.

I tried Doctor Herren first. His wife came down the stairs—ponderously large in the dimness.

"The doctor is not home," she said sharply. "Try somebody else!"

I knew this woman was lying, but I was poor.

As the door closed on me, I stood for a moment, not knowing what to do. A man skirting the stoop came up to me and asked where I was going. He lit a match to look at my face.

"Go to hell," I told him and sped across the street.

I got another doctor—a young, sympathetic doctor—who asked for the short cut to my home. As we walked, he tried to ease my tautness by inducing me to talk. I cursed God, charities, doctors, and their lying wives. At first, the young doctor at my side laughed, but when he perceived that I meant every word I said, he let me talk until I stopped of my own accord.

We came into our street.

A policeman on the corner swung his club. A cat ran light-footed down into a cellar. Jennie the Bum was going home with laggard footsteps.

Two hours later, my brother Daniel was born. It was the morning of Decoration Day, 1913.

The Charity paid our rent while my mother was unable to work. Not long after, my mother told me that the Charity wanted to see me. The doctor was to examine me to see whether I was fit to go to work.

"They have a job for you stringing beads," she told me.

On the day ordered, I cut the first period (biology) and went to Twenty-first Street. At that time the Charity still had heavy iron doors and I looked at them fearfully before I could bring myself to force one open.

I told my business to a man who met me at the entrance and directed me to go upstairs. I seated myself in the midst of some women and men who were also watching for the doctor. There was such misery on their faces that I kept my own well under my hat. I hated myself for not being able to help them.

I felt their curious eyes on me once or twice, just as I felt the curious eyes of the employees of the Charity fixed on me in wonder. I did not look like an applicant. I wore a white middy blouse and a black tie—regulation wear at my high school two days out of the week. The straw hat I wore cost seventy-five cents. I had to wear one to school. My shoes were worn out, but clean. I had wiped them with a rag before I left the house.

"You look like a lady," my mother had observed defiantly, knowing it wasn't good policy to appear at the Charity neat and prepossessing. "But what they've given me before, they can give me now!"

Finally, a group, of which I was one, was called into the little anteroom outside of the doctor's office.

"Why, I didn't think you were one of us," a woman exclaimed as we got into the room.

"But I am," I replied with a smile.

None of the women returned my smile. They were a little suspicious of me.

"But you're so young. No older than my Bashe," the woman said. "You're not fourteen yet?"

I nodded.

"What do they want from *you?*" she asked. There was a fierceness in her tone that dominated the curious quality in it that at first tended to antagonize me.

"Work," I replied indifferently, still smiling.

Here a bowed little woman with a glass eye came out. She adjusted her shawl to her head as she passed us.

"Nervous, I am?" she said bitterly, addressing us all. "Nervous? I am hungry. You hear? I am hungry."

She shuffled out of the room, muttering to herself.

A tall, gaunt woman looked after her stolidly. Her black shirtwaist, open at the neck, showed each bone in her breast. The veins stood out prominently. Her face, taken from the rest of her worn-out body, would have made a striking death's head. Her eyes, black and without a glimmer of light in them, were sunken into her head; her pale lips were drawn apart and down. Even her large yellow ears, hopelessly abject, listlessly apathetic, stood a little away from her head.

Her husband, an expressman, had been killed in an accident by his own horses. There were children, of course.

She was called in next.

When she emerged, she was feebly trying to run her tongue around the corners of her lips.

"What did he say?" asked the woman who had questioned me.

"He said I was nervous," was the answer spoken in the Russian-Jewish dialect. She did not have to whisper. Her voice was but a shadow. You were conscious only of her "s." "He said I ought to give the children away and I should go to work. I'm nervous but strong, he said. I should go to work."

A swift gleam, like that of lightning, flashed for a moment in her eyes. Suddenly she tore her shirtwaist and showed us her breasts. I hid my eyes. When I looked up again, she had gone.

Then I was called.

At a desk, writing busily, sat a man of about thirty-five. Perhaps he was more. His black hair, parted on the side, was oily and lay in place obediently. He wore glasses and his dark face was unshaven.

"Well, take your blouse off," he said to me.

I opened my tie and loosened my middy at the front.

Dr. F. looked me full in the face, impersonally cynical.

A hurried, perfunctory examination—tapping and listening to the beat of the heart and my answers to questions concerning the past state of my health.

He looked up at me with a well-intentioned smile. Doctor F. should never have smiled. "Well, Bella, you'd better go to work," he said, familiarly placing his hands on his knees, elbows out. "You see, you're the kind that needs work. Education isn't good for you. You're too nervous—too high-strung. Work would be just what you need. You couldn't make four years of high school—you're too nervous. You know that as well as I do. From your answers alone, I could tell that you're nervous."

I had a great inclination to laugh—but to laugh so that everyone in that house of stone would laugh with me. But I didn't. I mechanically made up my tie and went out.

"What did he say to you?" The women crowded around me.

"He said—I was nervous."

At least they laughed with me, but only our eyes heard that laughter.

Not long after Danny's birth, we decided that we were going to get rid of "Der Lange" (the Long One). This boarder owed us for three months rent and there didn't seem to be any sign of his ever paying for one.

My mother found the excuse when "Der Lange" slept until one o'clock and showed no desire to rise.

"Get up, it's after one," my mother said to him.

"Shut up," he told her sleepily.

A half hour later my mother said, "You'd better get up. I'm tired of having to clean after you when I should be earning a penny."

"What'll you do if I don't get up all today?" asked "Der Lange," opening one eye slightly. His tone was, "There, I have you. You can't do a thing to me. You're afraid of me. I'm a man and you're only a woman."

My mother considered a moment before she replied. "I'll call a policeman for you."

This seemed to enrage the Long One to such an extent that he jumped up in his bed, the quilt caught up around his belt.

"You'll call a policeman?" he said, bouncing up and down the bed. "You slut! Who are you, anyway? Get out of my sight before I trample you down! A policeman, she'll call!"

My mother and I listened in mingled amusement and fright. As the man showed no signs of stopping, my mother ran down and came up with a burly looking man who immediately stepped up to the bed and ordered "Der Lange" to dress himself.

He did as he was told, whining the while. When he was ready, the official-looking man ordered him to get his things together and get out of the house. "Der Lange" whined again but got his belongings together and left us.

My mother thanked the man before he escorted our late boarder down the stairs. She told me later that she had been unable to get a policeman—none being in sight. But on seeing this big man—"he does look like a policeman"—she had asked him to come up and help us.

Another boarder, just as lazy but not as lively, was David, a tall, blond, handsome boy of twenty-four. David was cursed with a mania for poker. He rarely won but he always played. He never kept a job for longer than four weeks at a time. If he wasn't fired by that time, he left of his own accord. In the late morning, more frequently the later afternoon, he would rise, stretch himself noiselessly, and advance to the sink for his ablutions. With his fingertips, he would reach hesitatingly under the water and then sprinkle himself with a few drops. Quite seriously, he applied the towel.

In front of the looking glass, he would stretch himself again, running his long fingers through his hair as a supplementary action. At the door, he would stop because my mother would be saying, "David, when are you going to pay me last month's rent?"

David, squirming under the shadow of his felt hat, would not reply.

"I tell you, David, much as I like you for a boarder, I can't keep you if you don't pay. Haven't you even got a dollar—a half dollar, even a quarter?"

Sometimes David would have a half dollar and he would hand it over to my mother. More frequently he did not, and then my mother would tie him to the door knob, "washing his face" for not paying her promptly.

David was quiet and deferential, but he was a gambler. And a gambler never has money, my mother concluded, so he too had to move.

There was a third boarder I remember, who with a gay kerchief on his head, rings in his ears, and a sword at his belt would have made a genuine pirate blush at his own sorry appearance. Schloime had a thick, pendant lower lip, fierce humped eyebrows, and a hooked, hair-filled nose.

He told wondrous fairy tales and knew all the ghost lore that skulked though the midnight lanes of the home village he would never see again. Some of our boarders kept the memory of their old homes green with reminiscences of their boyish exploits or youthful endeavors or ideals. Toward that end, Schloime told and retold his fairy tales and ghost stories. He had a rapt listener in me and was crafty enough to use this to his advantage when my mother pressed him for his rent.

Schloime was not an idle fellow, but he could not resist a beautiful day any more than a child can a gay balloon. So that when lunchtime arrived (he worked in a shop where combs and tortoise-shell rings and bracelets were made) he usually forgot to return in the allotted half hour.

Most of his fairy tales were strangely similar to those that I had already read in the books I had gotten from school and the libraries. But they were more alluring as they rolled forth from Schloime's thick lips and now flashing, now somnolent, half-lidded eyes. That man was a caravan of many-tinted rainbows as he sat slouched against the dim wall, his hat drawn over his eyes, his lips painting pictures. First it would be the ghost of the miser who sold his daughter to a peasant who beat her and who therefore could find no rest in his grave. Nightly the ghost father haunted the scenes of his former home, until the daughter committed suicide by drowning herself in a well. Now people who are abroad at midnight can see the ghost daughter pursuing her ghost father until dawn chases them both back to Beyond.

The fairy tale that would follow told of the six sisters who were changed into stones because they had each turned out their old mother into the snows when she had rapped on their doors for help. The seventh one, who was to the eye as honey and milk is to the taste, had taken her mother into her own bare little home and had shared with her the milk and cornmeal mush that she and her husband ate summer and winter. When she spoke, roses, jewels, and gold coins with the King's head on one side, fell from her lips. The four lived together thus in great splendor and happiness. When the old mother died, six white horses drew her hearse to the river's edge.

For these and their like, I would intercede with my mother when Schloime would make excuses for nonpayment of rent. But my mother had to ask him to go one day when he absentmindedly put another boarder's coat on underneath his own.

How we ever achieved the rent when the day of payment came around, I don't know. Invariably, my mother would have to beg a few days' stay. The landlord, still a young man, had already acquired the calculating glazed look which all of us on the Lower East Side understood as "Pay or get out."

He never looked directly at us.

I remember one hot day, at noon, I had put Herschey into the cradle and Danny lay in the bed, also in the front room, when Mr. I., the landlord, was expected.

I was bending over the babies' tin bathtub, washing diapers and dresses for the next day, when three sharp, short knocks sounded.

I had barely formed "Come in" when Mr. I, trim and cool, stood at the door. He never advanced into the apartment— always at the door. I sank my hands deep into the muggy water.

"Rent?" said Mr. I.

"Rent?" I repeated after him, stupidly, as if I did not know what he wanted. "My mother isn't home, but as soon as she comes, I'll tell her you were here," I hurriedly said. My hands hurt at the wrists.

"She can give the rent to the janitor."

"She'll bring it to your office," I faltered. My mother's relations with the janitor were not of a cordial nature.

The landlord's figure had, if it was possible, stiffened until he looked like a tailor's dummy.

As soon as my mother returned, I told her of the visit of the monthly *malach ha-moovis* (angel of death).

"I have six dollars for half a month," my mother said with a smile of triumph. "What a pity he didn't come when I was home. A great pity."

That summer Herschey began to walk. I trained him on the corner of Houston and Goerck streets and down on the Third Street pier. When he would go to sleep in the carriage after his noon egg and glass of milk, I would race over the cobblestones back to the house to fetch Danny.

My mother would be at the sewing machine, her back to the squalor that was our home. First seeing that Danny was dry and fed, I would pick him up and race back with him to Herschey.

With Danny on my lap and Herschey asleep, I could read at the same time. During that summer, the undersized children of the bowlegged plumber on the block fished out an incomplete paper copy of Tolstoy's *Resurrection* from a garbage barrel and brought it to me. In return, I bought a penny ice-cream cone and presented it to them.

When Herschey would awake an hour or two later, he would sit up and delightedly jabber to my brother Danny, who responded equally well. Frequently women, and men too, would stop and unashamedly stare at the two in the carriage. Pregnant women looking at Herschey's disfigured face would stick their thumbs in their belts* and immediately look away.

One woman, whom I had seen frequently on the block, laughed out loud on seeing Herschey. The black salve that I had applied in the morning was still on his face. "Look at the little rat."

For a moment, I felt as if the roaring in my ears and the pounding within me would never stop. Then I walked over to the woman and struck out. My outstretched hand landed on her neck.

That woman never again stopped near Herschey's carriage, but when she saw me, with or without him, she would cross to the other side of the street. As her revenge, she tried to spread the rumor that I was crazy, but the street chose not to believe her.

One night, after a particularly hard day with the children and at home, I could not sleep. Events had been crowding in on me crammed with a heavy, misunderstanding hand. My mother lay at the head of the bed with Herschey next to her while I lay at the foot. Danny slept in the cradle. In the kitchen slept the boarders.

From the street lamp opposite a stray beam of light narrowed and widened together with my thoughts. Finally, I got out of bed as noiselessly as I could and went to the open window. The street was sinisterly quiet. A slight breeze paused at the window for a moment and then seemed to die on the sill.

I looked at the sleeping tenements and down at the street strewn with garbage and wet newspapers. Was this living? Someone moaned from the fire escape above me, some sleeper who had sought a little rest under "God's canopy." God's canopy! I looked up at it sneeringly. We could see enough of it to be able to believe that somewhere God did keep his canopy, but all we got was one thread from its many million fringes.

Four cats scampered from one side of the street to the other

---

*A superstitious custom used to guard against bearing ugly children. —B. S.

and waited, crouched.

And there was Jennie the Bum, coming out of a hallway, patting her badly dyed hair. I recognized the man with her as the son of a very pious white-bearded man and bewigged woman of the street.

It was all so hopeless. When would it all end? I began to drowse and dreamed consciously—that a vast fire destroyed the slums but no one was hurt. Everybody went to the country and there were no more slums.

Suddenly a loud shriek followed by another and another roused me. "Where is my *boyele?*" a voice demanded. Give me back my little boy."

My mother, instantly awake, jumped up from the bed, while below a knot of people gathered in the front of the next house. Gradually the story came to us.

A family who lived on the fourth floor had found it so hot that they decided to sleep on the roof for the night. So up went the father and mother and the children, including the youngest, a boy of five. During the night, the little boy wanted a drink. His eyes were still covered with sleep, and in his haste, he took the wrong direction and fell from the roof to the backyard.

Toward the end of the summer, my mother met a friend of hers, a Mrs. Goldstein, who said she could come and help her cook at a wedding which Mrs. Goldstein was supervising. Mrs. Goldstein, corpulent, pockmarked, gold-toothed, with a kind heart and an irritable tongue, cooked at resorts during the summer and in the winter at weddings and sometimes in restaurants.

This summer she had not gone to the country because of her promise to cook at a large number of weddings. My mother helped her. And on those nights she would be out, I would wait for her return until two in the morning. The next day we would have chicken soup. My mother had saved the heads of the chickens—the heads were not used—and from those heads we would have a delicious soup. Mother would watch Herschey fondly as she fed him, saying, "Isn't it good that I met Mrs. Goldstein? She should only live!"

Sometimes she would bring home pieces of fried chicken and raisins. At first, they were scraps from the table, but later, my mother grew bolder and hid two or three fresh pieces under her coat before she began waiting on the wedding guests.

But people didn't marry every day, and Mrs. Goldstein didn't cook for everyone who married, so that these occasions of chicken heads were few and far between. And thus our chicken-soup period came to an end.

During that summer my friends would come to me or I would go to them with my brothers. Usually toward four o'clock I would trundle the perambulator with the babies to Third Street where the girls met on the stoop of a vacant dilapidated house. There, I once read to them the most eloquent chapter from *Audrey* by Mary Johnston. Another time, for a week, we saved our pennies to go to the country. Sara Pellenberg had figured it out and announced that it would be quite possible if we saved consistently summer and winter for five years. At the end of the week, however, Clara Mill, who could imitate the crow of a rooster, took a penny from the fund. This was the beginning of the end.

Sometimes we would all go out for a walk, I propelling the carriage, my two brothers sitting up in it, the girls on either side of me.

My friends tried hard not to notice my brother Herschey's sores. They were kind, but sometimes one would forget and it would hurt terribly, for I loved my suffering, backward boy more than anyone else. For several days afterward, I would shun Third Street and remain on my corner alone.

On other days and nights, when the heat was such that men and cats exchanged pitying glances, Sara and I would trundle my two baby brothers down to the Third Street pier.

Here the stench of still, slimy water would come up to mingle with the occasional breeze. Residents of the neighborhood sat on wooden stools and camp chairs they had brought with them, while others who came from a distance balanced themselves on the wooden embankment. In the daytime large trucks drawn by stout-footed, sweating horses would stamp onto the pier to unload lumber or big bursting bags from the moored boats. As this work progressed, the clean air would become vitiated by the smell of manure, spilled beer, and the brown pools of spit that the men dropped from their lips.

One afternoon, when it was so hot that even the workmen on the boats forgot to swear, I saw tiny little worms rise from the foot of one of the many wooden posts supporting the Roof Garden above. They looked cool and moist. And then there was the patter of running feet. Someone had fallen into the river.

At night, upstairs in the Roof Garden, a blaring, blustering band would play everything, beginning with "The Star-Spangled Banner." Around the room, going in one direction, strolled men in their shirt sleeves with their girls or wives. Young boys reveling for the first time in the possession of a straw hat led their sweethearts by a timid hand. Children, washed and unwashed, with or without shoes and stockings, circled their way between the couples, devilishly deriving pleasure by spoiling the pleasure of others. Sometimes in the far corners of the Roof Garden, fights would crop up, but the music would drown out the noise and soon the quarrels would be quelled by a policeman.

I would rarely go up but would stay below just outside the pier. Sometimes Sara would be with me or I would be alone. Then I would wonder and build tales around the golden gleams that lay parallel and remote from each other. I would sometimes think of them as the hands of the dead who had drowned. At other times they would become the jewelry which these dead took with them. And when I saw callow smoking boys spit into the limpid, golden curves, I shut my eyes.

At other times, when I felt nauseated by the stagnant fumes of the pier at noonday, I would wheel the creaking perambulator to the Hamilton Fish Park on Sheriff, and Houston, and Stanton Streets.* There was no covering of any kind to keep the sun off, so while I swung Herschey in the little baby swing, Danny sat in the heated sand gorging himself with it while the sun beat upon him.

When Danny's turn would come, Herschey would leave the swing with bad grace. He also ate sand, but his tastes were a little more delicate. He chose the finer sand and ignored all the pebbles.

One day, after a series of misadventures, I sat down on the curb of an unfamiliar street and cried, to the mystification of my two brothers and the curious interest of a dozen bystanders. When I had started out at noon with the carriage, one of the wheels had fallen off. To repair the damage took all of my strength and mechanical ingenuity. As soon as the wheel had been replaced, I found that Danny had wet himself and that I had neglected to take an extra diaper. Back I had to go for two others. I had to wheel the carriage in a certain way, for the refractory wheel was still of a mind to go its own way, and progress was slow and difficult.

Finally I found myself in the park and a partner to a fierce quarrel. Two of us claimed the same baby swing and a fist fight looked imminent. Just as I was ready to put Danny down into the carriage, to defend myself against my cross-eyed opponent, another baby swing proved vacant, and peace was restored.

Herschey, as usual, went first. Today he had developed a bit of swing fright but he would not get out. He just wanted to sit in it. I let him, giving him a little push at intervals, for there were

---

*Hamilton Fish Park, at the far eastern end of Stanton Street, is now bounded by Celic Plaza (Pitt Street) and Gustave Hartman Square (Houston Street). Sheriff Street would appear to have been overlaid by Masaryk Towers. —*R.L.*

mothers and fathers waiting with their offspring, and if they saw Herschey merely sitting and not swinging, they would have reported it to the park teacher who would have confiscated the swing. Finally I got Danny into the swing and Herschey took his place in the sand. Danny had been in the swing but a few minutes before I saw to my dismay that Herschey had gotten sand into his eyes.

I did the best that I could without any clean water, but the little fellow was in pain and I had to hurry home. On the way home, both of the boys began to cry and the rear wheel again fell off. This time I did not stop to put it back again, for it meant the collecting of a small crowd who would probably stare and laugh at Herschey, so I practically carried the carriage and the boys home. (It was a lie calling that place home.)

When would it end?

Poor as we were, the girls I knew felt drawn to us. Of evenings they would come from Grand Street, quite a distance away, and from Third Street and Avenue B, to our house.

If we happened to be in luck that night, I would go down and get three cents worth of "skin." Skin was the back of the smoked salmon. On this some of the smoked salmon was still to be had, and if I were fortunate, I might fall heir to a piece of skin that was worth four times as much for the pieces of salmon still on it.

I would simply cut up the skin in as exact a proportion as I could and hand them out to my guests who would all be sitting on the bed. Without more ado, they would fall to, and soon the skin would be a limp, lifeless thing, while the diners would be crying for water. We never had too many cups and glasses, so they would have to wait their turn.

Once, the dwarflike children of the bow-legged, black-eyed plumber (those who had given me *Resurrection*) brought me a harp. It was really a zither but I liked to call it a harp. It still had two or three strings left. I accepted and thanked them. They—

there were three of them, the oldest ten, then eight, then six—withdrew behind several barrels for a discussion and then announced to me that I could pluck the "harp" with a fork.

I thanked them again.

That night, the girls came: Mary, her sister Bettie, Clara, Lena, Sara, Rose, and several others. Herschey and Danny were elected guests of honor. After the skins were passed around, the harp was played not only with forks but with spoons. Each girl had a turn. We did the balcony scene from *Romeo and Juliet:* one girl draped in an old skirt of my mother's and a boarder's old felt hat, the other, Juliet, in a shawl which fell from her head.

Danny and Herschey played "soft music" on the harp.

Romeo sat on a chair because she was tired, and Juliet stood upon the edge of the bed. It wasn't safe to stand on the spring.

After that, we had several original selections by the orchestra. The only instrument we had was the harp. My two brothers played that. All the rest of us imitated an instrument—violin, piano, cornet, flute, cello.

Before the girls left that night a vote of thanks was offered to the absent three sons of the bandy-legged plumber, the donors of the harp. Attempts were made to do it in Latin, but when failures seemed to be the only result, the girls happily recited:

> *"Mica, mica parva stella*
> *Miror quaenam sis tam bella"**

substituting "plumber's princes" wherever possible.

It was a hilarious time.

After the girls had left, the house looked more desolate than ever—even with the gas turned low.

---

*A doggerel version of "Twinkle, Twinkle, Little Star," sung or chanted by generations of beginning Latin students. It is worth remarking that the curriculum of the New York City high schools included Shakespeare and Latin. Students preparing for college would also have studied a second foreign language—in Bella's case, German. —*R.L.*

Danny slept in the bed, his round face prettily flushed, while Herschey slept in the cradle flaccidly hugging the two-stringed "harp."

A day came when we could not pay the rent. We were handed the regular dispossess notice and my mother began to run hither and thither, to the Charities, to the boarders who had left owing her money, to philanthropic women on the East Side. When she got home, her eyes gleamed in her yellow face and she was wet to the skin.

"There's nothing," she said wearily. The picture of our furniture in the street and the tin plate must have appeared to us both, for we seemed to see the reflection in each other's eyes.

For once, that hope with which we lived from day to day flickered—and went out.

"Let me go to work," I suggested, "then everything will be all right."

"No, not while I'm alive," my mother shouted. "You're going to be a lady. Not like me, a *schnorrer!*"

That night we slept as if dead.

But the next day, my mother rose with new determination and a heartening flush on her sunken cheeks. I kept the children in the house, fearing the neighbors' looks.

When the children went to sleep, I began to gather up the ragged clothing, shoes, and bits of stuff I knew my mother would not part with. I wished I could burn them, for it seemed to me that as long as we kept these rags, we would always be kept in our ragged, impoverished condition. The rags were to me chains and prison walls. But I could not, for we could still use this and that, and my mother would not part with her rags.

Our luck changed on the fourth day.

The Charities gave my mother fourteen dollars—seven with which to move and seven with which to pay her deposit. She found rooms on First Avenue and Forty-ninth Street and we were to move on the following day. They had also given her work: renovating worn clothes of the rich for the poor at thirty cents a garment.

"What kind of rooms?" I asked. I had never been to First Avenue and Fourty-ninth Street.

"What kind?" She had heard me well enough, but she was tired with much walking and weeping. "What kind do all the poor get? The same like here, but the neighbors there are people, not beasts."

"You told them—already—there?" I asked constrainedly. I did not like to refer to my stepfather even in the most roundabout way.

My mother hesitated and looked away from me. I knew she was going to lie.

"No—I told them nothing."

I knew she lied.

PART V

First Avenue

First Avenue to me seemed illimitable. I knew it began at First Street where the "L" swung in like a wild beast charging at the tenement windows, but just how far it extended never troubled me. For me, it ended on Fiftieth Street—except when I had to go to the Charities, when it ended on Sixty-second Street.

The street is a never-ending trail of truck horses and spilled gasoline. Wagons and automobiles clattered by our window incessantly. Only on Sunday did the noise cease and the street become strangely quiet, save for an occasional voice or one laugh answering another.

First Avenue on a Sunday in spring is what I remember best, perhaps because I want to forget the other days. The wide street with no manure in the crossing; the hint of green trees at Beekman Place near the East River; the families going to and from church, sleepily communicative; children's straw hats gay with colored ribbons gleaming in the sun; and a blue, blue sky.

But the street was not always like this. Only on a Sunday in spring. Other days, it was a restless, panting street with thin lips gossiping, gaping, grinning. A street that hurt since it turned its face away at the sight of my brother and laughed with covered-up mouth.*

The house we moved into was not different from the others we had lived in: four tenants on a floor, two toilets in the hall, two tenant families for each toilet; rent to be paid monthly or bimonthly. Sleep . . . eat . . . work. Sleep . . . eat . . . work.

We sat and ripped and sewed worn clothes which the Charity gave us to remodel for those like ourselves. We received thirty cents for each dress. We worked far into the night on the dresses, for both my mother and I wanted each dress to be different from the other so that the child or woman wearing it would not be ashamed of the style. I ripped, designed, sewed on buttons and buttonholes, and ironed the dresses. It gave me great pleasure, even when I was so tired that I could not keep my eyes open.

There we sat in our workroom, the gaslight burning brightly over our heads, while Danny and Herschey lay in the big white bed, breathing in the manner of tired sleepers. In the corner was our oak sideboard, partly covered by our work and by a glass pitcher on a glass tray surrounded by seven glasses, like a mother hen with a brood of chicks.

"Just listen to those two on the bed!" my mother exclaimed softly, stopping her pedalling of the machine. "One would think they worked hard in a railroad or building houses to hear them snore."

She stroked the left side of a ripped skirt with a forefinger, sighed, and returned to the machine with false vigor. A moment later she stopped again and shivered noisily.

"Oh, how lonely it is here!" she cried. "Not a man or dog on

---

*What Bella Spewack describes are the slums and abattoirs of Dead End and its environs. They began to be replaced—elegantly replaced—in the 1920s. The area was not fully gentrified until the United Nations buildings and gardens were built following World War II. —R.L.

the street. No lights, no people, no laughter—at least downtown you see people of your own kind—and they're alive—but here, it's like a cemetery. And I feel so alone."

The following week the Charities discontinued the work, giving as its reason that we no longer belonged to the district. We were transferred to the Bethel Sisterhood.

One Monday, my mother told me that the Bethel Charity wanted to see me. It was as if two stones had been placed upon my eyes. The old fear of humiliation began to cut me with a keen, shining blade. They would ask me why I didn't go to work. They would look at me and whisper among themselves. They would nod their heads while their eyes would point at me.

"I'm not going," I said sullenly.

My mother looked at me with begging eyes. "You want they should stop the rent?" she asked. "Things are going too well for us? You want I should run around to people and beg?"

"Oh, I'll go to work."

"Over my dead body will you go to work. You're going to be a lady, Bella, not like me a servant, to be ordered around by clumps of mud."

My mother lit the gas under the pot of coffee. "Don't offend them, Bella. Be nice and respectful. They're giving us our rent. Where would we be without them?"

I went.

On the street, I met the idiot errand boy of the neighborhood coal dealer. He smiled at me and drew his maimed little arm closer to his side. I looked away.

I entered the gray stone building.

Something within me felt like a book being closed and opening rapidly, creating little gusts of wind that chilled me through and through.

One moment, I felt afraid. And the next, I wasn't.

There were others in the hall beside myself—a few women. An office opened out at the left side of it; straight ahead was a large dark room whose size I could only guess at.

115

I felt a large woman looking me over. Her head sank into her round-shouldered back. She wore a white apron under which the tips of her shoes protruded—flat and round. She folded her arms over her breast. Her head sank further down between her shoulders.

I don't remember what she said to me. Perhaps she said nothing. I knew that she despised me, however. My fear should therefore have grown, but it did not. People were beginning to interest me for themselves and not so much for their relation to me. It was not because I had grown stolid.

I felt another woman looking at me—a small, frail, hatted woman who wore black. She smiled to me. I looked at her. I was not quite sure that she was smiling to me. Sometimes people smiled through me. At me.

I returned the smile warily.

She had had me called because my mother had said I needed shoes. The resentment against my mother flamed out again.

Miss Neslow—the woman in black—led me to a door further along the hall and to the right of it. It opened on a dark room which smelled of camphor balls, shoes, and paper. The gloom gave way to light and I could see that this was a store-room where clothes were kept for those who needed them. The suits hung neatly against the wall and the shoes were disposed of on the shelf along the opposite wall.

"You must never go without a hat," the soft-faced little woman in black said to me. "It isn't ladylike. And you might get neuralgia. Have you a hat?"

Her voice was a lovely undulating drawl and reminded me of cream-colored old lace I had seen rising and falling at the throat of a teacher in school.

"You need shoes," continued Miss Neslow, looking doubtfully at the high-heeled pairs. "You can have the heels cut down, but that would spoil the shoes. You'd better take a pair until someone sends in others that are low-heeled. I'll set them aside for you."

I felt mystified. Never before had such kindness and courtesy been mine from a charity source.

Miss Neslow's manner emboldened me to select a pair of shoes for myself. She looked at them and then at my feet and shook her head doubtfully. I removed my own shoes and slipped on the others. They fitted.

"How strange," murmured Miss Neslow, "you are really very poor and yet you have such small hands and feet."

I smiled apologetically but the book inside of me began opening and shutting again.

After watching me try to wrap my "new" clothes up, Miss Neslow pushed my erring hands aside and silently did up the bundle for me.

"Really, you'll have to learn to be a better packer than that," she observed with a smile when the bundle was in my arms. "You'll never get a job in a department store on that parcel."

"I want to go to college," I said stiffly and turned blindly for the door. Then I remembered that I had not thanked this kind, unimaginative woman, but somehow the words would not come. I stretched out my free hand, caught hers in mine, and held it for a moment. It was a daring thing to do.

Out in the hall, the large woman who had looked me over was holding a round-faced baby in her arms. She was smiling at it. On seeing me, she resumed the grim, suspicious manner with which she had greeted me, just as I was about to approach and thank her for—for the rent and the clothes.

I am at home with the things I have received: some children's clothes, a brown suit, a white shirtwaist, a black velvet sailor hat with a silver ribbon (how I have longed for a silver ribbon), and a pair of shoes with high heels. I immediately put the rompers on the boys. I dress myself in the suit, the skirt drags on the floor, and I clap the hat on my head. My mother wears the white shirtwaist and the four of us gravely walk up and down the front room. I bow to imaginary acquaintances.

The children are asleep with my mother. I am alone with my books. Suddenly, I drop my head into my hands. After all, they are charity clothes. I have no right to be so happy.

My neighbors began to assume living shapes for me.

Over us lived the O'Connors, a drinking widow and her two little girls: one, a crooked-mouthed cripple, the other of the conventional Irish type. Both went to school. On Saturday nights, their mother had company. On Sunday, the little cripple went to church with a blackened eye.

Next door lived the Nemeroffs: an industrious, unintelligent, swarthy Jew who collected fat remnants from retail butchers which he sold to soap manufacturers, and his family consisting of his wife, Bluma, and three children. Bluma was a frowzy-haired matron who, rather than wash, ran her husband into debt buying new things for her offspring and the house. Her voice reminded me of the times you attempt to break a piece of soap when your hands are wet. Just when you give up, the soap breaks. So with her. She would speak for three minutes running in a low, tongue-tied monotone—and then suddenly stop in the middle of a word. She was known as Bluma the Lazy One.

Below us lived a Scotch family. The mother, who always wore a hip-length black silk cloak, was regarded as mildly insane and was rarely seen on the street; the husband was never seen, not within or out of the house. There was a very pretty daughter with narrow blue eyes and bangs touching her black eyebrows. I saw her when she came home from her work—her hips swinging freely, her eyes demurely hidden from admirers. On the same floor with them lived a noisy, oil-smelling Italian family, an old Jewish couple, and the Jewish janitor and his family.

On the third floor lived the suave Rabinowitz with his equally suave wife, neighbors to the O'Connors. I disliked her on first sight. She was too interested in our affairs and wanted to help us too soon. In the back lived round, red-cheeked Becky, her father, who had a big voice and heavy black brows, and her silent white-haired mother who wore large diamonds in her ears and on her gnarled, thin-skinned sallow hands. Becky was sixteen. It was said her mother was jealous of her beauty.

The fourth floor was practically owned by the Murphys: the old Mrs. Murphy, who worked in a department store though she was the grandmother of a girl of twelve; her daughter Kitty, whose face was like the silly little dogs some childless women carry under their arms; the younger Mrs. Murphy, who drank spasmodically without the bacchanals Mrs. O'Connor indulged in, and her husband and her three or four children. Another Scotch family completed that floor, the Hurleys. I never saw them except on Sundays, when they all went to church: a grizzled, square-faced, tight-mouthed man; an oily, red-faced woman of meek mien, who always looked overheated; Agnes, an eleven-year old carrying her sand-colored little head tightly between her shoulders—her way of looking proud; a pug-nosed, grim-faced boy of thirteen; a fair-haired baby with a wet, gray nose and stone blue eyes.

Below us, next door to the silent, brooding Scotchwoman, lived an old couple—they were so old that to me they smelled of the earth. So dark were their three rooms and so musty with the odor of the aged that it was like having the door of a coffin close in on me when I entered.

I ran errands for the old woman. She was a tall, narrow-shouldered, broad-hipped woman with little smudges of deep-seated dirt near her wrinkled nose and at the corners of her webbed eyes. She very rarely went into the street. Her windows were always shut. I doubt whether they ever could open. Everything she wore was black or as nearly black as continual wear can make brown or dark blue. She must have worn five or six petticoats, even on the hottest days, and the effect of her moving across the floor was like that of a round-bottomed boat. Her feet never appeared—it was the front part of her dress that seemed to propel her.

Old Mrs. Trow had one vanity: her wig. Every two months or so she would sound a spoon on the water pipe, which would be the signal for me to go down. The wig would be waiting for me in a paper bag. Mrs. Trow knew of a widow hairdresser on Ludlow Street, on the lower East Side, who worked cheaply. I would be given my carfare and twenty-five cents for the errand and dispatched to the widow on Ludlow Street. On those occasions, I would take Herschey with me. Sometimes when I would take Danny, Herschey's reproachful eyes would follow me to the door, and then I would come back and comfort him and kiss him.

Several months after we had moved to this new place, Mr. Nemeroff, husband of the shiftless Bluma, became my pupil. I was to teach him how to sign his name. It seems that he suffered great mortification when a business associate in the course of the day asked him to sign his name and he could respond only in Yiddish or with a cross.

"Now, if you'll learn me to sign my name so—" with a circular flourish of the pen in his hand—"I'll make you a present that your eyes never saw before."

Mr. Nemeroff had a triangularly shaped face, with the chin sticking out several inches from his collar. Naturally of a swarthy complexion, the dirt and grease which, as a driver, he collected during the day made him considerably darker, until sometimes in the uncertain gaslight, I would wonder if this were really Mr. Nemeroff or some stranger from Morocco.

From the first, he refused my suggestions of learning with a pencil. It was to be pen and ink or nothing. What was it my concern if he broke pens with his boorish hands? So long as he could pay me fifty cents for two lessons a week, could he not pay a cent or two for a new penpoint? Mr. Nemeroff loved to boast of his prosperity.

Frequently I would have to remind him that if he did not attend to his ABCs without further reference to the butcher whose wife had a harelip, or to the murder on Forty-eighth

Street, he might as well not be spending his money. Sometimes his wife would appear after knocking with assumed timidity. There was a man waiting for Nemeroff, an old friend whom he had not seen for a long while. Would he come in and not keep the guest waiting?

Mr. Nemeroff would rise and run his fingers through his closely cropped thick hair—an action which he thought eminently suited to a learner, a student like himself. At times, he would wave his pen in the circular motion of his toward the door, which he wife understood to mean that the guest as well as herself was dismissed. But Mr. Nemeroff was a sociable soul and more frequently he would wipe his reeking pen on his sleeve, go to the door, and look shamefacedly back at me.

"An old friend from mine country," he would explain in a sort of abbreviated English. "Tmawra make big lesson."

He would turn an eager face to his wife to observe the effect his English had on her. A lazy smile illuminated the good woman's freckled yellow face.

Her hands were clasped over her stomach while her feet, enclosed in dirty white "sneakers," stood far apart at ungraceful angles to each other.

"She stands like a water carrier," my mother once said of her.

Summer that year arrived with a brassy intensity. When a breeze came it brought with it the smells from the slaughterhouses further down the street. Cooking odors formed an impenetrable suffocating sheet in the narrow airshaft. Our home, always shameless in its poverty, became more wretched. We hated the sight of the enameled bed that had been bought so joyously before Herschey was born; of the little grey-white bed from which the paint was peeling—Herschey slept there by day and I by night; of the twenty-year-old mirror with its black spots crawling over it like so many spiders; of the sewing machine on which the installments had not yet been fully paid.

One day, after I had wheeled my brothers into the dark bedroom to escape the heat, my mother brushed away the faded blue dress she was altering for an Italian widow and rose abruptly.

"I'm going downtown," she said. "I got a plan. I know a man whose sister owns a summer resort in the Catskills. Maybe she'll give me a job. I'll beg on my knees for her to take me. I'll work for nothing if she'll let me take the two boys along."

"Tell her I'm big for my age," I suggested. "I can work too." The idea had taken hold of me as well. I saw green hills and bottomless skies.

My mother returned, worn out but radiant. She had met the proprietress herself who had consented to take us. She would pay our fare but no wages.

Mother was to work in the kitchen and clean the rooms.

We went the following week. My mother and I took with us an old valise that some boarder of the Goerck Street days had left behind him. My mother carried Danny, her corsets, and a bottle of hot milk for Danny. I carried Herschey.

I felt irritated with her for not having put all her bundles together, for I saw people stare at us and snicker. My irritation turned to resentment at these people who knew nothing but to go to the country for their pleasure every summer. I scowled at them and bit my lips to keep from crying.

I saw several women rise ostentatiously and walk down the train toward us to gape at Herschey. Herschey was lying in my arms, sick. He had fallen ill the night before, but we feared to delay lest the proprietress change her mind.

My mother did not appear to see the curious glances that came our way and the hurried consultations of the high-breasted women. She smiled often to me and I tried to smile in turn. But I could not. I felt if I smiled, I would burst into tears. And then those Argus-eyed women would have a chance to come up close. I could even visualize that the one with the many diamond rings would try to raise Herschey's eyelids up so that she might see his eyes.

"Why don't you smile to me? Give me a little laugh," my mother pleaded anxiously. "People will think that you are angry with me."

But I could not. I kept my eyes either on Herschey's blotched little face or turned toward the window.

"Look at the way Danny's eyes are getting bigger and bigger," my mother persisted. She thought that would make me smile.

"Don't," I said stiffly. "Don't. It's no use, I can't." The tears welled up into my eyes and went down my cheeks. I caught them with my free hand. "Do you think it's fair that you should have to work when all these women are going out to play? Do you think it's right for Herschey to lie here sick when all their children are well and happy?"

I stopped—suddenly, it must have seemed to my astounded mother. I had seen the woman with the diamonds whispering to her companion sitting opposite. Her eyes pointed at me.

I raised my head fiercely and shook the tears out of my eyes. But I couldn't give a laugh.

We arrived late in the afternoon. We had barely time to wash ourselves before my mother's employer came to tell her that her work was waiting for her.

"Could I have a little milk for the children?" my mother asked.

The woman nodded hurriedly. She was a tall, narrow-ribbed person with flaming red hair that looked as if it had never been combed, and a pair of green eyes that seemed as intimately freckled as her face. As she led my mother to the kitchen, she looked over her shoulder at me.

"Your daughter?" she asked. She had a harsh, masculine voice.

"Yes," my mother replied.

I knew what was in the red-headed woman's mind. She was sizing me up.

I forced a little warm milk down Herschey's throat and placed him on the bed. Danny was tired but energetic. He gulped his milk down quickly and signified his intention of exploring the neighborhood. I gave him a blade of grass and he fingered that wonderingly. I put it to my lips between my two thumbs and whistled upon it. Herschey opened his sick, burning eyes and smiled. Danny laughed with glee.

When I heard Herschey's weak little one-stringed laugh join Danny's lusty one, I again put my lips reverently to the bit of green between my thumbs. I wore out several blades of grass before my brothers were satisfied.

So when we were moved to a room smaller and closer to the hot kitchen, I did not feel dissatisfied. In it were two large beds. One had a mattress, two pillows, and a grimy, lifeless quilt. The other, which stood next to the uncurtained window almost facing the kitchen door, had no bedding at all, not even a mattress.

My mother and I exchanged curious glances. Where were we to sleep? Herschey lay in my arms and Danny lay on the mattressed bed.

Finally the red-haired woman appeared at the door. She beckoned to my mother who followed her meekly. It was a long time before my mother returned. In her absence, two other servant women had entered and asked me to take Danny off their bed. But I could not and so they waited in tired silence for my mother to appear.

At length she staggered in under a huge feather bed and a single pillow. The feather bed she smoothed down over the spring and the single pillow she placed at the head of the bed for Herschey to lie upon. With an apologetic glance at the two other women, she removed Danny from their bed and placed him at the foot of our bed, his head pillowed on my coat. My mother slept next to Herschey, and I next to Danny. We arranged the feather bed so that it amply supported the two babies, but my mother and myself slept on the bedspring.

The next morning, when the babies awoke, I went to the

kitchen and waited for my mother to approach.

"The children are up. I need some milk," I whispered to her. My mother nodded.

I went back to our dreary, fly-filled room and waited. After dressing Herschey and Danny, I let them play outside of the room. At last my mother appeared with two bowls of oatmeal, a pitcher of milk, and a plate of buttered bread.

Herschey ate part of the oatmeal and a piece of bread. My mother felt in her apron pocket and drew out two boiled eggs. I fed the eggs to the children. Their appetites were encouraging.

"You go in the kitchen and help yourself," my mother said. "I'll stay here for a minute. But hurry!"

I got some milk and oatmeal and bread and butter scraps from the diners' tables. To me, it did not matter. Outside of that hot kitchen, piled up with dirty dishes, there was a blue sky and a host of butter cups and daisies.

I finished as quickly as I could under the appraising eyes of the red-haired woman.

That day for Danny, Herschey, and myself was a memorable one. We traveled far. I took Danny on my back and Herschey in my arms as I walked over boggy ground. Several children belonging to the guests, to whom I had told a fairy story earlier in the day, came too, in the hope that I would tell them another. I did, but only after I saw them lose their fear of Herschey's grotesque little face. I was fierce with desire that children play with Herschey, for they shunned him and he loved them dearly. There we sat in the long grass, Danny and Herschey in my lap, the children around me, while I told them of Cinderella and the glass slipper.

When we got back, it was time for supper.

My mother brought the babies their little meal as surreptitiously as she had their breakfast and lunch. I accepted this as a part of the red-headed woman's kindness in letting us come.

"I'm afraid she doesn't like me," my mother said sadly. There were deep hollows under her eyes. We looked at each other, reading the question in each other's eyes.

"I hope she doesn't send us away," I said fervently. "Herschey's looking so much better."

My mother's eyes lit up. "If she'd only keep us for two weeks, he'd be a different child," she said eagerly. "I'd work my hands off if she'd let us stay."

The harsh, commanding voice of the red-headed woman calling my mother interrupted our hurried whisper.

"What must you do now?" I asked, as my mother rose hastily.

"The silver and the pots," my mother replied. "My thighs hurt so I can hardly stand."

"Let me go," I said. "I can do that as good as you." Before my mother could speak, I ran to the kitchen.

The red-headed woman said I did better than my mother. The appraising look in her eyes changed to one of satisfaction. "You're a good worker, but you're not fast enough," she said.

"Give her a chance," said one of the servants who had taken a liking to me. "She'll learn. She's only a child."

In my endeavor to please our employer I attacked the pots with all the strength that was in me.

"Don't work so hard," my friend of the kitchen whispered. "Let her work her own intestines out."

But I wanted her to let us stay and I doubled my efforts.

As I lay down to sleep I welcomed the cold bedspring touching my body. "She'll let us stay, I think," I said to my mother. "You see, both of us will work and she can't complain. Why, she's saving at least fifty dollars a month with both of us working."

But my mother did not answer. She was asleep, one hand protectingly cast in Herschey's direction.

The next day, we overslept, and the red-headed woman blazed with wrath. She was not satisfied with her investment. She was sorry she had told us to come. There was that sick child and that other healthy one who ate too much—and a big girl. The girl alone she wouldn't mind. But the others. . . .

The climax came with Danny's wetting the feather bed. The

red-headed woman would listen to neither of us. If my mother wanted to leave me behind, she would give me twelve dollars a month. But she wouldn't have my mother and the children, not if my mother spit with gold for her.

So we came back.

The tragedy of that return.

The morning following our return to First Avenue I went to look for a job.

"How dark it is," I kept thinking as the ads I had clipped from the morning papers turned into bits of pulp and my feet grew heavier and heavier, for this quest for a job had led me into streets that seemed still another world, where massive sheets of office buildings cast a queer, thick, hot gloom. The streets were clean and people ran—and ran. And I was a part of it. And so were the three girls I had met at noon. And the truck drivers with their great, lumbering wagons. And so were the pimply-faced errand boys with whom the girls flirted.

"We're gawn home, 't's no use lookin'," one of the three girls said to me. But I walked on to Bleecker Street and finally down Broadway until I struck West Houston Street. It was all so new to me.*

I watched two girls come out of a loft building. One of them looked at me—the taller one.

"Is there a job in your place?" I heard myself ask. The two girls looked at me blankly and then laughed. I laughed too. It was good to laugh.

"You've gotta nerve," the taller girl said with a shrug. "Y' think jobs come just for the askin'?" She smiled merrily. "Got experience?"

---

*The streets Bella was discovering were little more than a mile from the heart of the Lower East Side. That she viewed them as "another world" indicates the physical circumscriptions within which she lived. —*R.L.*

No, I had none. What was the work?

Again we laughed.

I walked with these girls in that hot, rushing gloom until they brought me back to the loft building where I had met them.

Somehow, I cannot remember their faces. They were a part of the gloom.

"Now r'member," they advised, "y're a little experienced, but last summer yuh worked on buttons an' yuh don't r'member so good. Now come on."

A gong sounded as we opened the door. We had no sooner entered the vast room with many long tables and benches on it than another gong sounded and girls of all sizes and ages, some with their aprons, others as if they had just come from the street like ourselves, rushed to and fro and gradually, like the pattern in a kaleidoscope, settled into rows of girls with nimble hands that worked steadily pasting flowers or branching feathers.

My two companions of the street were no longer with me.

I was alone.

A half hour later and I was a part of the pattern.

I was seated at a learners' table with silent girls of my own age. We received a pile of quills and stripped them, leaving a tuft at the tip which we snipped at with the scissors so that it formed a triangle.

All learners got three dollars a week. Girls not yet sixteen left at five; girls over sixteen at six. All girls reported for work at half past eight and there were thirty minutes for lunch. This I learned from my neighbor who lisped. On the second day I was promoted from "plucking" to pasting. I began to look around me.

My table was made up of about a dozen girls—some Irish, others Italian, and a few Jewish. The Jewish girls would teach the Italian girls lewd words and the Italian girls would return the courtesy. The Irish girls acted as squealing audience.

When spirits ran high, Mamie, the Irish forelady, would

walk up to our table and "speed" us up. The mere sight of her stopped buzzing tongues. She was small though large-bosomed with a snub nose, round, sharp, provocative eyes behind rounder specs, and a mass of red-gold hair piled high on the top of her head.

Several times during a day, the hand-organ grinder would stop on the street and play rolls of restless ragtime. Shoulders would begin to move imperceptibly and an irresistible hum would begin. The Italian girl who had spent seven years at this table would roll her eyes suggestively.

Then Mamie's resonant Irish tones would boom sarcastically. "Say, girls, this ain't a picnic!" Or: "Cut the rag out!"

I rarely had occasion to talk to Mamie, and she knew me only as "that high school kid."

On the third day, I began to cough. I could not sleep. When I was not coughing, there was a peculiar tightening tickle in my chest and throat that gave me no peace.

The next morning the Jewish girl drew her chair away from mine while the Italian girl facetiously asked me what wood I had chosen for my coffin. When I went to get a drink of water, however, she dropped her own work and pasted on mine so that I would not lag behind.

Mamie's scorn descended on us like a bucket of cold water.

Shortly before lunch, the little errand girl went the rounds of the table as she asked each one of us what we wanted from the street. A pear? An apple? Candy?

I shook my head. I wanted nothing.

At twelve, the gong hurled itself at my aching head. My one thought was to get out into the street where I could breathe. There I mingled with a group of girls who were eating their lunch of banana and bread in the street. Their talk came to me as through a mull curtain. Now and then I understood what was said—but only in blotches. Even listening was fatiguing.

Then the tall girl who had first befriended me drew me

aside. "I heard of a good place for you," she began. "Gotta do everything. Paste, strip, branch—go on errands, answer the phone, get lunch for the girls—do everything."

"How many girls are there?" I asked.

"It's a small place—"

"Don't you want it?"

"Me? Wha' fuh? I'm an experienced hand. An' I ain' gonna be no errand girl for nobody."

Within a minute, my determination was formed. If I hurried, I would be able to talk to the boss of this new job, and if he didn't like me, I'd still have my old one.

I went up to the tenth floor and entered through a door marked "S. Friedman, Feather Fancies, Feather Boas, Novelties." Two girls were seated at a table. One of them, even in the fleeting glance I could give her, was as lovely as a pansy. She was a Greek girl. The other girl was a Jewess with a troubled mouth.

A man with a very small face and an immense, hulking body was standing near a door that faced a little hall around the corner.

He turned about and looked at me. Then he took his straw hat off and tapped on its crown, as if in deep meditation, and put it on again.

"Experience?" he asked.

"Yes."

"Where'd you work?"

I told him.

"Bellah—uh-huh—Bellah," repeated the big man. "Well, Bellah, I'll give you four dollars a week. Start tomorrow. Get in by half-past eight." He waved an effeminately shaped and sized hand, plentifully freckled.

I got back in time for the final gong.

My new job was heaven compared to my previous one.

In the morning, I opened the establishment. It consisted of one room, the back of which was the workroom. In the foreground was a large, roll-top desk, telephone, chair and water cooler. This was the office. Close to the wall was a gas burner on which we made cocoa and coffee for lunch. During the day the burner was covered by a kettle of steaming water. You dampened the ends of the feathers with the steam before you curled them.

The girls would get in, always with fresh news of the night before. If they had not seen each other since Saturday, they would not begin working for ten minutes. They had so much to say to each other. What did you wear to the island? How was the water? Who were you with?*

At ten o'clock, Mr. Friedman would get in with a brisk "Good morning."

"Did you get the ice in all right?" he would ask me. It was my first rite to wash the ice and slip it into the cooler. Then he would turn to his correspondence while keeping up a steady stream of comment.

On the afternoon of the first payday, Friedman called me to him. He sighed powerfully as he swung round on his swivel chair.

"Bellah," he said, "I'm afraid I ain't got the money to pay you. Can you wait?"

I felt as if I'd been struck in the face. "Not even two dollars?" I faltered.

"No," shaking his head lugubriously and sighing. "I'm going out of business. Your four dollars a week is too much. . . . Could you, maybe, work for three dollars a week?"

"Why—if—if," I hesitated.

Mr. Friedman continued, mournfully, "I'll look in my pocket. I have a dollar, I think. I hope it'll keep you until I can get another one—" fishing out a bill—"Why it's a two dollar bill and as I live, here's another!"

---

*The reference is to Coney Island, an immensely popular working-class playground. —R.L.

Here Josie and Fannie burst into loud laughter and I laughed too—after a while.

Josephine, the Greek girl, and Fannie, the Jewish girl, were both fast friends. The boss's business was a matter of frank discussion between them, and I soon learned that Mr. Friedman had married a second time—that his wife henpecked him. That she held the moneybags. That he played up to her.

One day when we were just finishing up an order for a buyer from Peoria, our boss's wife put in her head at the door with a cheery, condescending, "Good afternoon, girls." She was a small perfumed woman with a veil flowing from her hat.

Josephine, who sat with her back to the door, stuck her tongue out, while Fannie murmured, "She means good night."

We had been working all day, barely taking time to eat our lunches, because this was a rush order.

Behind Mrs. Friedman, stood our boss, an apologetic, blinking figure.

Mrs. Friedman advanced to Josie and placed her hand on her shoulder.

"Don't do that," said Josie grimly, "you tickle me!"

"Who's that girl?" asked Mrs. Friedman, pointing at me with a parasol.

"That's Bella," said the boss, without his customary facetious reference to my hundred and one duties in his firm. He looked troubled.

"Bella," she repeated vaguely. "She look like Frances Goodheart's niece, doesn't she?"

Mr. Friedman nodded. He nodded vehemently. I felt sorry for him.

"Girls," began Mrs. Friedman, in a brisk tone, all the sweetness cleaved from it, "I want a feather boa—black and white—curled."

"For next week?" demanded Josie.

Mrs. Friedman laughed coyly. She tapped Josie's shoulder with her gloved index finger. "No, darling, tonight!"

It was nearly five at that moment.

"You mean tomorrow morning," Josie returned coolly.

Fannie was busying herself putting the kettle on the burner. She was a kind-hearted girl and she did not wish to see the red rings of heat and nervous exhaustion spread around the pleading little gray eyes of her boss. Putting the kettle on was the signal to Josie and me that Fannie for one had decided to make the feather boa for Mrs. Friedman.

And we did. Mrs. Friedman sat at her husband's desk toying with a blotter and remarking how terribly hot it was, wasn't it?—hottest day she'd ever seen!

"It'll be hotter when she goes where she belongs," muttered Josie to me. Her usually soft, moist black eyes were narrow with suppressed fury.

Mr. Friedman walked back and forth. For the first time, I noticed that he stooped, that his pepper-salt suit bagged at the knees.

I was dampening the feather boa over the top of the uncovered kettle when a sudden jet of steam scalded my arm. A stinging pain made me cry aloud. But I kept the feather boa in my hands.

Mr. Friedman stopped his pacing and looked over inquiringly.

"I burned myself," I explained apologetically.

Josie's eyes softened with pity, while Fannie rose with a sigh and took the boa from my hands. She examined the burn. It was shaped like a leaf and stood out red and breathing. "Don't touch it," she said wearily. In a lower tone, "When that cholera gets out, I'll fix it up for you."

At seven, two hours after our usual closing time, the feather boa, neatly boxed, reposed under Mr. Friedman's arm.

"Good-bye-uh," said Mrs. Friedman with a gracious incline of her head.

Because of my injured arm, I was assigned to sorting out a

deep box of feathers, putting those of the same color, quality, and size in individual boxes. It was pleasant work.

As if Fannie were swinging in a tree high above me, I could hear her telling of her mother's latest symptoms. Now, her droning voice came forward—now it receded. Fannie was waiting for her mother to die, so she could marry the man who had been waiting for her ever since she was seventeen. She was now twenty-four.

Yes, it would be pretty . . . a brick-colored ostrich feather on a black velvet sombrero shape. I fingered the bit of feather and placed it in its box.

Fannie's voice . . .

"The doctor came but what can he do? Nothing. He comes and we pay him. Sometimes I think it's cancer, but I'm afraid to ask and he won't tell me. Sometimes I imagine myself saying: 'Doctor, is it cancer or what?' but I never do. Before you have time to say a thing, he's got his satchel in his hand and he's on the other side of the door." A sigh . . . an old woman's sigh.

A sky blue feather . . . only dolls should be permitted to wear sky blue feathers in their hats . . . no living person.

"So he says to me, 'Fannie, what's the use of waiting? Ain't I waited long enough? Let's get married simple and quick. Your momma'll never die. She'll always be sick like she is.' Every night it's the same. Comes night, comes him and the same talk. And he's right. I know he's right. But I ain't got the heart to marry him with a dying mother in the house. . . ." (Josie's voice very far from me mumbled something.) "I know. Believe me, I know. He'll marry somebody else and I'll be left with gray hairs in my head. But honest, I can't keep him tied up no more. I said to him how many times, 'If you see a girl you like, and who likes you and you want to marry her, go marry her and be happy, I'll send you a good present.'" (Wiping her tears with the back of her hand.)

I was not sorry when Josie's plastic tones reached me. This time, I was on the red feathers, ranging from cerise to wine.

They fitted the shades of her voice.

For the most part, my program for the day was not interrupted. At half past eleven, I would put my work aside and ask the girls what they wanted for their lunch. Sometimes they would have brought theirs with them and then they would simply ask me to get them fruit or candy. When they didn't, I would get a "coupla" sandwiches or can of baked beans, or spaghetti. We each had our cups and saucers and spoons. To me, the fact that I had my own cup and clean dishes was another source of my belief in my ultimate "respectability."

I do not know whether I can make it understood how the thought that I was a "charity case" was always with me—how it never left me. Constant charity investigation had made me sensitive. Yet when I ate my lunch in the shop from my own cup and saucer and spoon I felt free and "respectable." At home I always felt that so long as the Charity paid our rent and had a right to investigate us whenever they wished, I was not respectable. I couldn't be. It was a barter. In exchange for the rent they paid, they took from me my self-respect. Then I called it my "respectability."

The rest of the summer my workday was just one feather fancy after another, relieved by the intimate confidences that Josie and Fannie exchanged over butterfly hands.

When the time came for me to leave and go back to the high school, I left the dishes behind me. I felt that it was not right for me to take them home. They were symbols of a thing that neither my mother nor I possessed.

On my return to school in the fall, I found some part-time work with Mrs. Slazens. Once a week, I helped her maid with the cleaning of her apartment. Mrs. Slazens had been my student club directress.

Here I found two hours of uninterrupted peace.

At first I felt a little confused. The luxury of the place excited me. Gradually, under the influence of the broom and the cloths with which I cleaned the windows, the rhythmic motion of my arms soothed me. Before the two hours were up, I had finished my work and could wait for Mrs. Slazens.

Then I would dream with the beginning of night, as the lights appeared on the street. Around me was a pleasurable warmth while the windows I had cleaned reflected a clear, frosty sky of ever-deepening blue and gray.

One morning following a day I cleaned at the home of Mrs. Slazens, my mother called to me to wake up.

"Herschey is sick," she cried. "Feel his head."

I sat up quickly, for I was accustomed to being called at any time when my brother fell ill. Herschey's head was indeed hot. So were his little hands. The doll-like feet were cold.

"What did you give him to eat?" I asked.

"Nothing. Just a little roll and butter and—"

I broke in with a short laugh. When my mother was preparing to lie, I could not be patient.

The doctor was called. As he wrote his prescription, I could see his eyes resting knowingly on the signs of poverty. My mother hovered anxiously about and followed him into the hall. I heard her continued, deferent babbling and then the sound of the doctor's footsteps on the stairs.

"He has a heart, that doctor," my mother said on returning. "I gave him the dollar you made yesterday. Now I'll go and get the money for the little dress and then I'll pay the drugstore."

At the door, she turned to me wistfully. "I'm sorry to keep you home from school, Bella, but I'm all alone—when you're not here to help me, I'm like one lost."

That night, Herschey's fever left him and my mother blessed the doctor and his powders. In the morning, Herschey opened his eyes and called to Danny. But he was thinner and smaller. Each attack, slight though it was, took with it a little of the tiny boy's strength.

In between these illnesses my mother listened to advice of all kinds. One day, it would be baths of milk, which we could not very well afford. Another day, it would be baths of water in which pigs' feet had been boiled. Frequently, I would go to a stable on Forty-eighth Street where I would get hay and straw for still another kind of bath. Then our rooms were heated to the sweating point and the door locked so no one could enter while Herschey was in the tub.

My mother spent all we earned tracking "professors" to whom she told our story, but these wise men could do nothing for my brother. How he would shrink from their touch as his sick little eyes called to us.

During a brief respite from our worries, I decided to make my bedroom look less like a closet and more like a real room. I cut pictures from magazines of James Whitcomb Riley, Robert Louis Stevenson, and Rudyard Kipling, and mounted them on the backs of old blank book covers. One of Maude Adams I bound clumsily in a six-cent frame—my only picture in a frame.*

I could not help boasting to my friends of the wonders of my room. But when they saw it they called it the Black Hole of Calcutta. My room had no windows.

My mother was always subject to schemes by which she would at last regain her self-respect. I turned a deaf ear to all of these until one night, not long after I had acquired the Black Hole of Calcutta, she could stand my indifference no longer.

"You don't care how long the Charities eat me up!" she exclaimed wrathfully.

I had many times explained that all schemes needed money

---

*Another example of the English curriculum offered to immigrant children. Bella would have learned of Maude Adams, however, from newspapers. The actress was famous for her performances in *Peter Pan*. —R.L.

with which to be carried out. And we had no money. I went on translating my Cicero.

"Yes, my friends are right," my mother stormed. "You are selfish. They say once you get your education, you'll be through with me. Put that aside and listen. Books! Books! I shall burn them all. You're throwing your mother away for books. Whoever heard of a daughter doing that to a mother? A mother like you've got! How many of your friends would wish to have a mother like me! I'm sending you through high school."

"You're not," I interrupted bitterly, "the Charities are."

"The Charities!" my mother flared up anew. "The Charities! Why if it wasn't for me, they'd tear you to bits. It's me, your mother, that's sending you with tears and blood. It's me!"

I raised my hand for her to stop. There was an examination the next day, and I needed every moment I could keep awake in for preparation.

My mother saw my hand go up and before I could shield myself, she was at my hair, pulling it and scratching my face. Suddenly, I felt her go limp. I opened her shirtwaist, gave her a drink of water, and then, wiping the blood from my face, I went into the street. There was a drugstore nearby that kept its lights burning until twelve. I sat there with my Cicero until eleven; then, feeling very stiff, I rose and looked for a time at the filtered radiance of the green and orange globes with which the drug-store filled its window corners. The lovely colors were reflected in the mirror that lined the window in the rear.

There I saw the gash at the corner of my forehead. It was still bleeding.

I turned and walked to Beekman Place. From behind a spiked fence I looked down on the black waters of the East River and felt a momentary peace. Then chaotic despair. Not even the mysterious lights that called could comfort me.

It was nearly twelve when I returned.

My mother greeted me with a slow raising of the eyes, and with a show of humility she set a cup of boiled-out coffee on the table.

"Oh stop it!" I muttered.

She caught sight of the blood on my forehead.

"I did that!" she cried, horror-stricken, wringing her hands, the tears coming to her eyes. "I did. Oh, Bella, Bella!" She was still wailing when I fell asleep.

I had not forgotten the appraising gleam in the red-headed woman's eyes, so towards the summer of 1916, I made up my mind to work in the country. Because of lunches and fares, I calculated that in the shop I usually earned a dollar and fifty cents less than the four dollars I received as pay. As chambermaid or waitress, I calculated on getting twenty dollars a month and my meals.

I thought these things over very gravely.

My mother did not want me to go. It detracted from me—as a lady. The deeper we sank, the greater was my mother's desire for me to emerge—a lady.

"Stay better home and take care of the children and I'll go to work," she begged.

I pointed out to her that I could earn more than she ever could.

Mrs. Slazens recommended me to a Mrs. Rosedell who owned a boys' school in the country and who was willing to employ me. My mother, however, wanted me to go to a summer resort which Mrs. Goldstein, our friend of the chicken head soup, had found for me.

"You'll get tips there," my mother argued. "And that's the very least you can do for me. Go where I want you to go."

I went up by the Hudson River boat. There was music and people's chatter and children continually exploring the stairs. It was all very soothing.

I was greeted by a brown little woman with blue eyes, who openly confessed her delight in my appearance.

"A little thin, but you'll broaden out," she encouraged.

I was chambermaid and waitress for her and her twenty guests for less than two weeks. I was compelled to go because I refused to eat the leavings of the guests.

My mistress screamed and raved and called me ungrateful and ignorant. She stamped about, a brown little woman wrapped up in her fury.

In silence, I went to the room which I shared with her and packed up my belongings. Then I walked out into the field to think things over. I had packed but where was I going? And then the absurdity of the situation overcame me and I lay down in the grass and laughed until I could laugh no more.

As I walked back, my determination not to go home shaped itself. I decided to telegraph Mrs. Rosedell and ask her if she could still use me.

The answer was for me to come immediately.

Back at the resort, I found my mistress had secured control of herself again, but I had no desire to remain. She shrugged her shoulders. "You'll be glad to come back here," she said. "The trouble was I treated you too well."

In the automobile, on my way to the dock, I changed from my own torn slippers to the high-heeled brown shoes a school teacher at the resort had given me in lieu of a tip. Making sure the chauffeur was taken up with the wheel, I dropped the old ones to the road.

I was ready for my next job.

The Rosedell school grounds and buildings seemed magnificent. They were so large and well kept. There was a tennis court—I had never seen one before—and a swimming pool and miles of trees.

I arrived just in time to take my place waiting on table. The one assigned to me was nearest the far end of the room. The first time I carried my tray laden with food for sixteen boys, the dining room seemed to measure a mile. It was exactly sixty-five feet. Sensitive at all times, I felt as if the two hundred and forty eyes in that long dining room were all fixed on me and all those ears were listening to the tapping of the schoolteacher's shoes.

At the end of the evening, I went up to my room in the servants' quarter near the top of the house and found my roommate undressing. She was a German, with a peculiar combination of stubborn silences and stretches of loquacity. She was sitting on the side of the bed.

"You are de new gurl?" she asked, her long, solemn face showing plainly that she preferred being alone.

I nodded and reached for my valise under the bed. The strange lightless eyes of the German girl followed my every movement.

"Where do you like to sleep—on the inside or the outside of the bed?" I asked her.

"*Können sie Deutsch sprechen?*" she said in reply.

"*Ja, aber nicht viel. Ich bin nur ein Student.*" I said.

In a moment, the stolid face lit up. "*Ganz gut!*" she exclaimed joyously. "*Ganz gut!* How long will you stay?"

"I don't know," I replied. "I'm very tired. I feel as if I could never move again."

"Pity!" Fräulein said in a whisper. "You should rest up before you again begin work."

"What do you mean?" I leaned on my elbow.

"Forget to get up tomorrow and I shall tell the Fräu Rosedell that you are sick. That all last night you groaned and that you ought to have the doctor," my bedfellow explained easily.

"Oh, but I couldn't do that. It's not honorable."

"Ehrlich!" repeated Fräulein with a short laugh that ended in a sigh. "You are young. When you are my age, you will think of what I say to you now. Nothing is dishonest or ignoble which gives you strength or keeps your body healthy. Close your eyes and I will do the rest in the morning."

Still protesting, I fell asleep.

The next morning, I arose, every bit of me aching with fatigue. Under the direction of Gertie, an ox-eyed girl who waited on the table nearest mine, I succeeded in laying the plates for breakfast. The trays seemed even heavier than those of the night before. Twice I stumbled, and a stab of pain cut at my eyes.

The Hungarian cook, whom I dubbed the Moon Lady because of her round face and round, nearsighted eyes, peered at me sharply.

"Say, leetle one," she said kindly. "You seek?"

I nodded miserably. My arms creaked under the burden of my tray. The good woman glared at me for a moment, then took the tray from my hands. "You take in tha t'ings one and one," she said.

I took in a bowl of eggs on my try and returned for the dishes and later for a fresh supply of bread. As I swung into the dining room, I could hear the Moon Lady's irate voice: "It is a shame for such a little girl to have to work so hard. If she were my daughter, I would keep her home and feed her eggs and milk."

I managed to clear my table, and since it seemed to be my turn to sweep the floor (the Scotch girl had said so, and she was the head waitress) I obediently dragged the broom about the room. I set my table for dinner and went out to the servants' dining room.

Here there were pitchers and glasses of water to fill, milk to fetch, butter balls to make, bread to cut, and other things which the diner always takes as part of the tablecloth.

In the dazed, painful way that I prepared for the dinner, I could still feel the impressions that my co-workers made on me, in an exaggerated, intensified manner. My mind was like a black piece of stage drop and all these busy men and women working at my side bits of red or green or blue pieces of paper that dance to the tune of an unseen fiendish fiddle. I felt this more and more during the serving of the dinner, the hardest meal of the day. There was the heavy soup tureen and the thick soup plates, and the meat and the flat plates and the dessert, and the milk and the salad. Would those boys ever stop eating?

The Moon Lady regarded me sternly as I held on to the

kitchen table to keep from falling.

"Go upstairs and sleep," she said.

Obediently I climbed the three flights of stairs, drew the blind down in the heat-packed room, and fell into bed. Tears of exhaustion relieved me of the tautness of my mind, but the physical pain would not leave me so quickly. My head throbbed irregularly, and the cough I had contracted in the feather factory the year before recurred viciously.

I awoke from a terrified sleep on feeling some one bending over me. It was Fräulein. A smile of approval lit up her grave, mourning face. For some reason she was pleased with me. I look up at her, puzzled.

She bent down to me and whispered, "Very good. Very good! I knew you would take my advice. I told the Fräu Rosedell how I heard you groaning and moaning last night and she was very sorry. Very sorry."

Fräulein twisted her features grotesquely to imitate the sympathy of our mistress.

I turned to the wall.

"You are a very good actress," commented my bedfellow admiringly. "But you will have to do even better. The doctor is coming right away."

I tried to tell her that I was really sick, but it did not seem important enough.

Fräulein clasped her hands in delight. "Oh, they will never tell that you are not sick," she breathed ecstatically.

A knock sounded on the door and Mrs. Rosedell, accompanied by a gentle, gray-haired man whom I judged to be the doctor, entered. Mrs. Rosedell was plainly worried, suspecting me of a contagious disease.

The doctor placed the thermometer under my tongue, took my pulse, and asked a few questions. Fräulein hovered in the background, her long face longer. She looked as if I were just one step from the grave.

The doctor prescribed some powders and advised resting as

long as possible. Mrs. Rosedell smiled in relief.

As soon as the door closed on our mistress and the doctor, Fräulein flapped her long arms and essayed several mild, jumping steps. She was dancing. "Oh," she gurgled, "you are the fine actress. You fooled even the doctor."

The tired feeling never entirely left me that summer, but after the first two or three weeks, I became adapted to my surrounding and grew less bitter. As I waited on these well-fed boys, who had had the good fortune to be born on the other side of the fence, as I caught glimpses of them on the tennis court, in the grove, in the pool, returning from hikes, working in their experimental garden, visions of the City of Dreadful Night interjected themselves between them and me with breath-catching suddenness.

At home, my baby brothers waited dry-mouthed for a breeze.

At times, when I could not go to sleep—the heat was so oppressive—I would build dreams to Fräulein's snores. I sent the babies and my mother to the country; I won scholarships; I went to college; was graduated with honors; achieved money and fame (very indefinite here). I even stood next to a charity investigator in a car and looked her straight in the eye!

But the occasions when the dining room was cleared for amateur theatricals, to be followed by a dance for relatives and friends, I was weighed down by a bitterness that could not be suppressed. None of the servants could participate in these festive nights.

Three weeks later, I was transferred from work as dining-room girl to chambermaid, although I was still a waitress. I was grateful for the change, although it meant harder work and earlier rising. It was still dark when I opened my eyes to peer half-heartedly through the window, to close them again in a passionate attempt to regain the sweetness of sleep; then warm feet on the cold floor and a helter-skelter sort of dressing with eyes half shut, vainly trying to dislodge sleep. I can still feel the wet chill of the dawn as I hurried to the big house, touching the wet green leaves as I passed. Green leaves are greenest in the dawn.

Daily I swept a long, long hall with broom and carpet sweeper. During the day I made up the boys' beds and waited on table. I was assigned to ten rooms, each containing two to three beds. On Friday or Saturday mornings, I would rise an hour earlier and scrub the hall, the servants' corridor and the stairs, and the boys' rooms. Finally would come the cleaning of the windows, when I could watch the sunset and the boys playing ball in the field.

Sometimes the boys would run in for a ball or a glove. Sometimes, too, they would stop to boast to me of their prowess or their wealth. Mostly they were just shy little fellows with shining eyes and abrupt speech. Then I would think of my own brothers and forget that Herschey was not like them.

Not soon after my change to chambermaid, I was given another and much larger room in the annex. The window faced the lawn and the room was much cleaner generally. Two others slept in that room with me. I found Margaret, the laundress, and another new roommate whose name I cannot remember to be a vast improvement on Fräulein, of whose eccentricity I had begun to tire.

Margaret's snoring was even more stertorous than that of Fräulein, but I found that by tapping her vehemently on the shoulder several times, enough for her to understand that she was snoring, she would by a strange effort control herself. As Margaret's bedfellow, I found myself the recipient of a dozen favors. Frequently, I wanted to walk for five minutes instead of washing aprons for the next day, and Margaret would look down into the blueing water and say, "Run along, child, I'll hold the tub for you. But you gotta be back in ten minutes."

Whenever I could spare the minutes, I would fold sheets for

my benefactor. But it was nothing compared to what she did for me by giving me the solitude of sun-sheathed trees.

I liked Mamie, too. She was the waitress who had once been a cloak-and-suit model. Now with bedraggled skirts and torn shirtwaists, she still lived in the past of tailored suits and plumed hats.

Mamie had a rare way of telling ordinary happenings.

One Sunday afternoon as we were watching one of the Bohemian kitchen girls drying her black hair in the sun, Mamie began to sigh. "That was just how my sister Evelyn died," she said finally.

Margaret, who had just come out to see whether the sky could get along without the laundry, looked sympathetically interested.

Mamie caught the look and launched forth. "It was this way. Evelyn—she was the youngest of us all, and there were four of us strapping girls at home—she had the most wonderful hair you ever want to lay your eyes upon. It was long and thick and spread over her back and shoulders like gold threads. And she had a face that matched her hair, all pink and white with big blue eyes. We used to say to her when we got in late and the hall was dark: 'Evelyn, we don't need lights when your eyes are around.' And that's just the way it was.

"Turned eighteen she was when a young man and his mother came to pick out a lace collar and cuff set for a sister at home. Evelyn—she was in that department—Evelyn and that young man just had to look at each other and they knew they was meant for each other. You know how it happens. A look in the eyes, a funny feeling in the throat and a catch at the heart. Well, Evie, we used to call her Evie at home, she gets home that night and she says: 'Sister, a swell and his momma have asked me to come to the house tomorrow night.'

"'Where'd you meet that swell?' I asks, being as I'm the oldest. And then she tells me the story. The young man, he waited for her outside the entrance with an auto and she couldn't say no and she couldn't say yes before he had 'er sittin' on the softest cushions you'd ever want to sit on. He took her to a restaurant where one man in a frock coat looks you over when you're standing at the door and another takes you to the table and another asks you what you want and another brings you the soup and another the ice cream and another the finger bowl. Oh—yes, I knew those places." (Mamie's eyes began to fill reminiscently. Mamie cried easily.)

"'Well,' I says, 'Evie, you're sure that this young man means the right things by you?'

"'Of course,' she says, 'I'm to meet his mother tomorrow night.'

"Well, when a fellow asks you to meet his mother right off, it certainly does look serious. And it was. The mother just took to our Evie, took to her from the first.

"'You're not at all like a department store girl,' she says to Evie.

"'No,' says Evie, 'my sister Mamie brung me up. And she's as refined a lady as you ever want to see. And my father didn't always have to work for his living. He had a stable all his own once.'

"That young man, he kept coming to our house and nagging Evie to marry him and finally she said yes. She held out as long as she could, but she loved the young man and she couldn't hold out no longer. Well, they made a date for the wedding, and we didn't see our Evie for days at a time. She and the young man's mother was shopping for the trousseau.*

"I says to Evie, 'Evie, you take a sister's advice and rest up.'

"And Evie listens to me, but she didn't get a chance to rest until one day before the wedding. Then I made her lay in her bed and I gave her breakfast and her lunch just as if she were a princess. And then I says, 'Evie, I gotta run out to fetch the

---

*To rhyme with Caruso. —*B.S.*

things for the supper. You go to sleep like a good girl.' Evie says all right.

"Well, when I come back, there was Evie sittin' in the back yard drying her wonderful hair. She washed it when I went out.

"'Evie,' I says, 'get in this minute. You'll catch cold.'

"'No,' she says in her sweet voice. 'It ain't dry altogether.'

"And she wouldn't come in. It was awful for me. When she got in, I acted mad and then she put her arms around my neck and she had me right away. No one could be mad with Evie. About four o'clock, Evie says, 'Sister, I'm sick.' I put her to bed and I went for the doctor. He looked at Evie and shook his head and he gave her some medicine. Evie was red and talking to herself, and her lovely hair was spread out on the pillow like as if the setting sun had been sitting on the foot of the bed." (Mamie's tears dropped into her lap.)

"The next morning Evie died—died on her wedding day."

Mamie pressed her handkerchief to her eyes and swayed convulsively. The innocent cause of the recital, the kitchen girl, was winding her braids tightly around her head with an incredulous smile. Margaret patted Mamie's shoulder with her always damp pink hands. She could say nothing to her but she was deeply moved. Finally she turned away and went back to her washtub. The kitchen girl walked off slowly in the direction of her work, patting her soft braids into place. Old Anna and myself were left to linger with Mamie. Anna kept her wary old eyes on Mamie's face and once or twice let them rest on mine in a significant way. She was trying to tell me something with her eyes, but I could not read the message.

Finally Mamie arose and smoothed down her apron. Without a word or a glance to either of us she went into the laundry from where we could hear her walk up to her room.

Old Anna shook her head, her lips forming grim, suspicious corners. "I guess you swallowed that story, eh?"

I nodded in surprise. It had never occurred to me to question it.

"Huh—" said Anna, as we both caught sight of Mamie advancing toward us. She had come down to get a shirtwaist of hers hanging on the line.

Anna eyed her craftily. "And did the young man ever marry after Evie died?" she asked innocently.

"No," replied Mamie gently, her hands resting on the clothespins, her eyes looking into the distance. "No, he never did. He loved Evie too much to marry. Poor Evie!"

Another Sunday afternoon, we servants went to look at a house in the vicinity belonging to an actress. In the group was Mamie, Ellen, a middle-aged seamstress, Margaret, the laundress, old Anna who, lumberingly waited on the last table following mine, a young, square-faced Swedish girl, and the two blond sisters, Frieda and Martha.

As we walked, now shifting from one partner to the other, I could see the women merging out of their cloak of servantdom. Margaret, whose rheumatic feet plodded hopelessly from washtub to line and line to ironing board, slapped Anna on the back and dared her race with a cripple. Old Anna refused with a shrug and a smile. She wouldn't race with a cripple but she'd watch an Irish reel danced by an Irishwoman. So there and then on the dusty road, with old Anna clapping her hands and myself whistling the tune, Margaret lifted her skirts and began the first intricate step of the Irish reel. In and out clumped the stump-shaped feet raising little swirls of dust with each movement. She was so happy—even when the pain of the unaccustomed exertion began to make itself felt.

Then the Swedish girl, whose silence made me call her Daughter of the Walls, volunteered to sing a native song. She had a monotonous voice nor did any one of us understand the words, but somehow we enjoyed it. As we stopped to rest, the shy little seamstress offered to show us how they danced in her Swiss village. She sang her music and danced a queer little waltz of many hops and skips.

In this way, we finally reached a tiny red and brown house hidden behind a circular group of trees. It had many shining windows on whose ledges rested green-painted flower boxes with no flowers.

"So, that's where she lives," observed Martha.

Old Anna laughed.

"And sure," said Margaret, "anyone could be an actress livin' in a wishful house like that."

"Her town house, they say, is grand like a palace," observed Anna, strangely proud.

"Oh—well," sighed Margaret, "there are some as has too much and some as has too little."

The Swedish girl, who had been peering at the sun with a shading hand, announced that it was time to return. So back we walked never stopping.

The boys of the school knew nothing of our lives. We were the servants who washed their clothes, cooked for them, waited on them, cleaned their rooms. We existed only as tennis balls, rackets, and bathing suits did.

I did not feel this until one morning, while cleaning the top of a dresser, I childishly attempted to draw a picture on the boy's piece of fungus. For the moment, I felt that I was not one of the chambermaids at the Rosedell School but a silly girl—past sixteen of a truth—but silly.

The mood passed. I turned to my beds, and as I was patting the pillows into their upright position, a little boy entered and seeing his piece of fungus stopped short and began to cry.

"Who did that?" he bawled.

"I did," I replied. "I'm awfully sorry."

The boy flung himself out into the hall. I heard his crying recede from me and then return louder and louder until again he faced me, accompanied by a counselor.

"Who did it?" the counselor asked.

"The maid," bawled the boy, "she—the maid did it."

"I'm not a maid," I cried out, angered. "I'm not a maid. Don't you dare call me that."

The boy and the counselor stared at me.

One of the maids had acquired identification.

The first week of September the school closed and the boys were sent home. Several of the huskier servants were retained to clean the buildings, but I wasn't chosen. I had hoped I would be, not only because it meant additional money but because it would keep me away for a few days longer from the home I dreaded.

I wanted to see my brothers but I didn't want to see my mother.

In the city, I found that no streetcars were running. They were on strike. I took a bus and parted with a half day's wages.*

When it stopped on Forty-second Street and Third Avenue, I got off with the rest and looked around me, dazed and indifferent. Big, lumbering, swearing wagons and auto trucks pass me, shaking the ground on which I stood. Lights, yellow and white, broidered the avenue with here and there the garish purples and reds of the moving picture theater. Children played near the curb lifting wilted heads to their lethargic mothers.

I picked up my valise and began to walk to Forty-ninth Street.

I felt that I had returned to a walled city, a city whose sordidness none could escape. As I walked up the dark, warmly damp stairs, I felt that the walls were coming closer and closer—that soon they would crush me like a huge nutcracker. At another moment, I felt as if my clothes were on fire and that I was running in panic, thinking to stop the flames that were stealing up to my neck. Yet I knew as I ran that the fire was enveloping me—that I could not escape.

---

*Unlike the nickel fares on streetcars, elevated trains, and subways, some bus fares were set at ten cents a ride. —R.L.

In the dimly lit hall, I was passed by a woman whose sole top garment was a shirt that smelled of sweat, tucked into her skirt. I did not have to feel disgusted as I did. I had come back to what I had left, to the Murphys, the O'Connors, the coal man's idiot with his warped hand, the now weeping, now laughing Sohlims of the rear.

I had come back.

I stumbled to the door which I knew opened on my home and turned the knob.

I turned my head and saw a woman at the sink staring at me, still as if I were a stranger. It was the woman who had passed me in the hall—she who had brought me back with her sweated shirt.

"It's you?" she asked wonderingly. "How big you've grown! To think I passed you like a stranger."

She dropped the pot she was washing with a ringing clatter and put her wet arms around me.

"You are home again!" my mother cried. Her tears dropped on my neck.

I could not return her embrace. She seemed to be near the walls and I was deep within the space they guarded.

I turned from her and looked about for my baby brothers. Danny, pale and fagged but well grown, stood up near a basin unconcernedly scooping up the water and letting it drip through his fingers.

"Where's Herschey?" I asked.

"He's hiding." My mother smiled. "He wants you to look for him."

And then he ran out from underneath the table and held up his arms to me. I took him up and held him close to me and he buried his head in my shoulder. He seemed lighter than ever. I could feel every bone in his little body through the thin dress he wore.

Then he lifted his face to mine and I saw that one side of his face smiled but that the other stood still, with the eye in it crying drop after drop.

"I didn't want to write you." My mother would not meet my eyes. "His whole side was paralyzed—now it's only that side of his face."

That night I wept for the side of my brother's face that would never smile again.

The feeling that the city—my part of the city—was shut in by inward-moving walls, that we, within, were suddenly dwarfed, did not leave me until I returned to school. There under the steadying influence of routine, things assumed their normal size and shape. But always, the walls were with me.

I took up my services for the old woman beneath us. My Latin teacher employed me in the stockroom and, after renting a typewriter for me, gave me some work for the department. In addition, I was correspondence clerk and bookkeeper for a boss painter and decorator. He did not pay me a definite sum but for two or three hours' work would give me a dollar and again only sixty cents. The painter was a stolid creature of moods.

Toward the latter part of the term, I became a kindergartner at the Beth El Sisterhood. One of their departments comprised the care of children whose mothers worked during the day. This included a nursery and kindergarten such as I had attended on Cannon Street.

The younger schoolchildren, those of six and seven, were my favorites. I would have them to myself for a half hour before the elder children arrived. They were docile things taught to obey and to wag their hands when they were questioned. They liked my fairy stories, and I liked to watch their round, shining eyes. But somehow they always remained as things to me.

When the children had been taken home by their mothers, I was glad to step out into the cold streets and see the little line of vapor issue as my breath challenged the frost. I walked rapidly, and if the streets were not snow-covered, I would skip and run part of my way. In fits of depression, I walked only and never lagged or stopped in front of window displays. Duty worked within me automatically.

Despite the student's fence that I had raised around myself, the worldly affairs of the tenement I lived in rushed between the gaps with dramatic force. I should have built for myself a stone barricade, but I doubt whether I can do this even now.

The school days rushed to a close with one Regents' examination following another; with girls exchanging sleepy glances and nervous smiles. And then came the blessed aftermath and the routine of receiving my diploma. The saying of good-byes does not stand out clearly to my mind; the anxiety for work overshadows it—but it was, I recall, vaguely sorrowful.

I began looking for work before I was graduated. I followed up every advertisement that held even the slightest possibility. I did this, I'm afraid, only halfheartedly. For I wanted to write. I wanted to write on a newspaper.

Simultaneously, I made the rounds of the newspaper offices, plowing through the slush and snow and returning home with nothing.

"It's good to have a home," my mother would say to me as I would sink into a chair near the stove.

Yes, it was good to have a home. But at home I had to think, and on the street I just walked.

At last, I was hired by a builder as typist and office girl for two and a half dollars a week, with the arrangement that I continue my stenographic tuition with a teacher whom he paid. The builder's office was within walking distance of my home so I saved on carfare and lunch. Altogether I felt that I had achieved a stroke of luck.

My desire to get on a newspaper did not die right here. I continued visiting the newspapers until one day a man advised me to try the local papers in the Yorkville district of the city. I could never get on a daily without experience.

It was a dim, low-ceilinged place—this office of the local paper—demarcated in the middle by a wooden railing. I approached a girl with shell-rimmed eyeglasses and asked for the editor.

A short young man who had been typing with the one finger method stopped chewing to say, "I'm the editor."

I looked him over, from his black derby hat to the third button of his vest, and shook my head.

"What do you want?" he asked.

"The editor," I repeated.

A tall young Irishman then arose from a desk near the window and approached the railing. "I am the editor," he said.

"If you are," I replied, "I want a job."

My coat at the moment was dripping little puddles to the floor. I had no umbrella. My toes wriggled uncomfortably in shoes seeping with mud. Impulsively, I placed my wet red hands on the railing: "I can write."

He took me at my word and hired me at space rates—that is, I was to receive three dollars an agate-type column, and expenses.

The first week I earned one dollar and fifty cents, then three dollars. That, with the two dollars and fifty cents from the builder cheered me considerably. Even my mother was happy. We felt that we were on the road to freedom.

But the third week there was no joy in our hearts.

I remember coming gayly home that night waving my pay in my hand. My brother lay in the big enameled bed, eyes shut.

"Herschey boy," I cried, bending over the bed, "Herschey boy, I got seven dollars for the country and ponies and a new suit."

But my brother did not hear. His smiling eye and his weeping eye were closed.

"Herschey boy."

The eyelids fluttered and one of his thin baby hands tried to lift itself up to pat mine, but fell down lightly into place again.

For four weeks he lay thus. Four weeks my mother dragged doctors and "professors" to the white enameled bed. Four weeks she did not change a garment nor did she sleep more than a few minutes at a time. I worked day and night for doctors and medicine.

Yet neither doctors nor my mother's "professors" could arrest the tightening of the little face, and as the face tightened, so did the body, until my brother looked like a baby of six months.

Somehow, as I come to the end of this, I want to hurry every sentence I write. Perhaps it is the doubt in my mind: "Have I said anything?" But it is more probably the pain of prying open my coffin of memories. My hurts make me run for I seek peace for my mind.

At nine o'clock of the evening of that night, my brother Herschey died.

"Breathe into his mouth, breathe into his mouth!" my mother cried to me. "You are strong. You are young. Breathe into him. He loved you."

I pressed my mouth to the cold little one and breathed into it.

But Herschey was dead.

My mother cursed the Charities and begged God to destroy them, for had they not destroyed her suffering child by refusing him aid?

"I asked them to send him to the country," she cried. "But they said he was sick. He would make the other children sick. He slept with his brother. Did he make him sick? They always said he should die—that we'd be better off without him! It's easy to talk away the lives of the poor."

My mother rocked back and forth, her short black hair falling about her face.

Suddenly she sprang up.

"You—you—" she cried, turning to our Irish neighbors who

had crowded into the room. "You pray in your churches. You must avenge the death of my child. The Charities took him from me."

During the night, I watched at the side of my brother. We could find no man to watch.

All through the night I held the icy little feet in my hands. Perhaps. . . .

My mother was mad with the pain of her loss. She sat in her mourner's corner and sang to herself. When my brother Danny toddled toward her, she pushed him away. When she looked at the shrouded looking glass, she covered her eyes with her hands.

"Oh, what my eyes have lived to see!" she moaned.

So it fell to me to arrange for the burial.

I went down to the free burial society on the Lower East Side where, in a large room, sat three bearded men sewing shrouds.

One of them, the smallest, came in the afternoon and washed my brother's tiny body in the little tin tub where he had played just four weeks before. Then a Hebrew prayer was said and the body was placed in a shroud much too big for my brother.

A hearse stopped outside of our house. A noise of crying women and subdued voices sounded in the halls. The coffin was brought up. My brother was placed in it. The men nailed the cover down.

My mother, and I, carrying Danny in my arms, attempted to follow the hearse on foot for we could afford no carriage. But the hearse moved swiftly. Herschey was light.

End.

Afterword

Lois Raeder Elias

B ella Cohen Spewack added the subtitle "Why I Wrote Comedy" to her book *Streets*. It's not clear when she came up with that subtitle, but in 1922, at the age of twenty-three when she wrote *Streets,* she didn't have comedies in mind. In fact, she was about to review an early life filled with anguish, fear, and sorrow.

Bella had written articles, poems, and many short stories, but never anything so ambitious as an autobiographical novel. At the age of twenty-three, that's not surprising. The unusual thing is that she understood that her life experiences as an immigrant child of New York City's Lower East Side ghetto was important enough to record. As with her reporting assignments, she approached writing about her own life with candor. The Bella of *Streets* is real. All the pain is there, and so is the laughter. Like some of the country's greatest comedians who came out of impoverished backgrounds, Bella was funny. Her wit could be excoriating at times, but her quickness and spontaniety is so surprising that you can't help but laugh.

If only Bella could have scrolled forward to the palmier days

159

when success was hers, she might have saved herself from the "financial furies" that never, ever left her. Survival was the name of the game from the day of her birth, on an unknown date, to an unknown father, and a soon-to-be immigrant mother. There is enough courage in Bella's story to take one's breath away.

Why should it matter that one little Hungarian immigrant girl fought with every ounce of talent that she had to survive? Her life story is duplicated by the stories of countless other immigrants. But no two people are alike, and very few people have the gift to take others along with them on their life's journey.

The turn of the century was a period of enormous ferment, and nowhere more so than in New York City where the changes were palpable. The flood of immigrants from the Old World began to give the city the multi-ethnic character for which it is famous. The melting pot designation may have been a misnomer, but the vast numbers of people who poured through New York's open door gave rise to a country that offered then, and offers now, unparalleled opportunities. This was the time when the character of the country was being forged.

Bella tells of her personal experiences as an American-in-the-making with such vividness that we cannot help but be grateful to her for her fierce zest for life and her determination to make the world sit up and take notice. And take notice it did. For Bella Cohen Spewack did more than merely survive. She became a recognized reporter (at a time when women were scarce in the field), an unusually imaginative press agent, a Hollywood scriptwriter with a wacky sense of style, and a Broadway playwright whose works are performed worldwide to this day.

Hints to Bella's future success can be found in the Prologue to *Streets*. Bella mentions that her mother, in the first conscious moments after her daughter's birth, reached out to implant dimples in her baby's cheeks. It might seem odd that Bella should make a point of something seemingly so insignificant. But not really. One thing that always stood Bella in good stead was the pleasure she took in her own attractiveness. Bella's dimpled smile, her strong teeth, her tiny compact figure were, for her, a source of strength. Throughout her life, the same awareness Bella took of her own presumed physical charms extended to her cultivation of attractive, talented, and successful people. In an interview with Arthur Greenspan for the *New York Post* when her husband, Sam Spewack, died, she said, "He was a very creative, wonderful, person. And he was still a very handsome man." By some uncanny instinct, Bella had a genius for spotting up-and-coming people of talent, as well as the necessary grace and self confidence to pursue the already recognized. She shunned the ordinary.

With the physical appearance of people and places so important to Bella, it is easy to understand that her writing style relies upon her keen observations. She wants us to see "the short, frail, blond man with the pink threaded cheeks" (4); the man with the "saintly, shadowy look of a prophet" (7); and "a widower with three children, who wiped his nose on his sleeve" (15).

These generally short, but very precise observations allow Bella to introduce us to an amazingly large and very colorful group of people. And we know how we are to feel about all of them. These neighbors and friends pressed in upon her from all sides. The ghetto allowed very little privacy. And if there was one thing Bella hungered for, it was elbow room.

Not only did the people crowd in upon one another, so did the smells. There were "the sugary odors of a pie factory," "the houses sour with the smell of so much crowded human flesh," (3) and school, where Bella "liked the neutral odor of the place" (21). If her adjectives told us how to feel about people, the smells suggest to us how Bella felt about her environment. The winner in every way, always, was either school, the library, or the country. What could be better when the smells are overwhelming than to have a place to go to where the smell is "neutral."

Bella's alertness to the physical aspects of the people and

places around her would prove to be a terrific asset. So was her natural ability to perform. And in *Streets* she was on stage practically from the moment she could prance about on her own. She exploited her cuteness in the beer gardens where, she says, "I would run errands for some of the actors and actresses and be paid liberally. I would imitate them and they would throw back their heads and laugh and I was happy. Very happy. I liked to make people laugh" (6).

Her acting ability became a device to protect her in situations where her youth and size might have put her at a disadvantage. There were the many Peckacha children who "all had great dark slimy eyes as if the gutter mud had been slapped into their faces and broad noses. They pinched me and slapped me just as they did to one another. Only when I 'acted' for them, did they give me peace" (7).

If Bella derived some pluses from her own performing ability, she was positively mesmerized by the gifts of others who could perform, like her Brightside Nursery School teacher, Miss Fannie. In "her striped blue dress with its white apron," said Bella, she "was to me the embodiment of all splendor." And when she touched the piano it became "a mysterious thing that cried and laughed" (11). Bella's ear, at nursery school age, was ready to hear and love music.

And then, there was the "Lovely Lady" who taught Bella how to sing "For Sale, A Baby." She was an actress and "had clear gray eyes shaped like a pear cut open, white skin, and hair the color of fresh apple sauce. Her teeth were white and she smiled often. She aroused all the romance in me because she was so lovely and because she was an actress" (21).

Because Bella's mother, Fanny, was a seamstress of sorts, Bella occasionally made the acquaintance of people who came from a world beyond the immediate ghetto. These strangers brought intimations into Bella's life of something out there that was not harsh and vulgar, unclean and mean. When Bella's mother insisted that she wanted her child to be a "lady," Bella could imagine what she meant. Around her she might see "a narrow, lightless strip that always smelled of conscienceless cats," but that wasn't all there was to life (44). Again and again, Bella made courageous forays into the outer perimeter of the ghetto, looking for something better than a "dry, baked street with its scattering of garbage in the gutter, the walls of tenements rising hopelessly on each side" (37).

The Lovely Lady who taught Bella a song was obviously not the first to notice the little girl's sensitivity to sound since Bella says that she could "sing well in Hungarian and German and spoke a broken Romanian, a smooth, declamatory Yiddish [and] before long could mutter realistically English oaths" (4). With Bella's theatrical capacity for mimicry, she played with the nuances of different accents, and when she needed to, could speak as well as any star. She could also write the sounds she heard. When Bella's mother speaks, we hear her. And Bella's friends had their own voices, as did her employers and co-workers.

The traits that set Bella apart from her tenement neighbors were nurtured to some degree by her mother, who appreciated her bright little girl, but felt hampered by her as well. Fanny Cohen was like any young single mother today, wanting to go out and have fun, but saddled with an "out-of-wedlock" child, whom she, and only she, must support. And what a child she was. Bella was a born fighter. In nursery school when the "red-headed boy of six who would get under the table and pinch our legs. . . . The girls always screamed, but would never tell the reason to Miss Fannie. When the boy pinched my legs, I kicked him" (12). That was Bella. She didn't tattletale; rather, she gave tit for tat.

One very specific difference that made Bella unhappy and set her apart from some of her neighbors, and all of her literary heroes in all the books she read in school and in the library, was not being a "Krisht." With her bright eyes wide open, Bella could tell that there was good reason to want to be a Christian.

"By dint of close observation I had made up the main difference between Krisht and Jew. Whereas the one wore gloves, the other did not; whereas one always had clean nails, the other had not; whereas the one never argued about paying children's fare on the trolley, the other always did; whereas one spoke perfect English, using long words whose meaning was difficult to render, the other did not" (29). It's little wonder that with all the beauty and goodness on the side of the "Krishts," Bella wanted to be one of them.

As much as Bella's mother might want to assuage her daughter's grief about being something she didn't want to be, Fanny either couldn't or simply didn't bring into the home any enlightenment about the meaning of being a Jew that satisfied her little girl. Occasionally, they went to synagogue, but her experiences there only reinforced Bella's desire to distance herself from other Jews.

One pious school friend, Edith Felks, helped Bella gain a somewhat more complex view of Judaism and even a grudging admiration for those who practiced their religion. Of all the friends Bella describes, Edith was the closest to her soul. Because the two girls were "as unlike temperamentally and physically as could be, our friendship took a long time to assert itself," said Bella (53). It's a blessing that the friendship eventually took because, as she said, "My friendship with Edith is one of the truly beautiful things I have to look back upon" (54).

Bella found in that quiet, religious household of the Felks family a calm that she seldom found elsewhere. And when Friday night came, Bella knew the quiet of that silent house would deepen; the family would draw together for religious observances and nothing would be allowed to disturb the Sabbath peace. Of course, Bella being Bella, she would have to tease her friend about their religious rituals, but she was nonetheless learning to appreciate the sincerity of a friend's identification as a Jew.

There never seems to have come a time when Bella actively

practiced her religion in any formal way. My husband, Arthur Elias, and I, during almost thirty years of friendship, never knew her to attend religious services. She did recount, however, having gone once to a Mikvah, the Orthodox Jewish ritual bath, with her good friend, the great actress of the Yiddish theater, Molly Picon. Even though she may not have participated in religious services as an adult, she always identified as a Jew, and donated generously to Jewish causes.

The strongest link between Bella and Edith was their mutual love of reading. Books were treasures to them both. Libraries were their joy. Over and over again in stories of impoverished youngsters, the public library was *the* place of refuge and delight. Certainly, that was the case for Bella and Edith. And, one of the pleasures in reading *Streets* is feeling the thrill that these two little girls experienced as they roamed the neighborhood discovering what they called "good" books.

In a time when children seem to be enamored of the television screen and computer games, it's refreshing to be reminded of the vast world of the imagination that books opened up to an earlier generation of new Americans. In all likelihood, reading remains the immigrant's gateway to learning. But with so many options available to children now that were nonexistent in the early 1900s, the power of the written word in book form may be less compelling. In Bella's immigrant experience, her intense enthusiasm for reading was without question a major key to her escape from poverty.

Not only did the public library open new worlds to Bella, but it put into her hands the first typewritten letter that she had ever seen—not just the first typewritten letter that she had ever received—but the first one to her knowledge that ever entered her home. Says Bella, "It had the letterhead of the New York Public Library, and it addressed me as, Dear Madam. Me, Dear Madam!" (55). Understandably, the girls were gleeful.

The beauty of Bella's storytelling ability, so exemplified by the girls' little exchange about a typewritten letter, is that you feel exactly as she feels. And since so much of life was difficult for Bella, these exultant moments provide a release for her and for the reader. Was this release a purposeful literary device? Possibly. The greater possibility, however, is that Bella had already discovered that dialogue was her natural domain. And she uses it effectively throughout the book.

And so was Bella's casting ability. Edith was perfect in the role of foil and dear friend. With just a very few words—"Edith gently insisted"—Bella tells us Edith was nothing like her (56). And she respected the difference. To Bella's credit, she had a sixth sense about people and an appreciation for the gifts of others that asserted itself over and over again in life as in her professional career. If the name of Mary Martin and many others came to shine brightly on Broadway, it was because of Bella's ability to recognize and reward real quality when she saw it.

Without Edith's supportive friendship, Bella probably would have pushed out beyond the boundaries of the Lower East Side on her own. But it was so much more wonderful that the two of them could go together in search of something out there, beyond the confines of the shabby ghetto. What could be more exotic than to visit the mansion that belonged to that symbol of wealth and privilege, Andrew Carnegie.

The girls never quite got as far as Carnegie's mansion, but they did get all the way to Fourteenth Street and Greenhut-Siegel's Department Store where they became literally entranced at the sumptuousness of it all. They even got up enough courage to chance the moving stairs. They must have looked like two little ragamuffins because on the third floor they encountered a guard who sent them packing. They left, but they left giggling. After all, they had had an adventure and discovered the moving stairs.

A word must be spoken about clothing. Throughout *Streets*, Bella describes ribbons, wedding dresses, silk petticoats, her own first silk dress (not really silk, but actually heavy, shiny lining material), hats, gloves, satin slippers with little buckles of white, and on and on. The one thing peculiar about all these descriptions of clothing is the mismatch with the subject and her own real-life, shall we say, idiosyncratic approach to fashion. There is no doubt that she had a singular sense of style, a certain panache. But she also was gripped with fear about spending money. And since she was a chain cigarillo smoker, her clothes were just as likely as not to be sprinkled with little ash holes. The dress would neither be darned nor replaced. A beautiful scarf, however, might be draped about her shoulders, as if that would draw attention away from the sprinkling of holes elsewhere. If the Greenhut-Siegel Department Store made a lingering impression on her, and no doubt it did, she never felt the same comfort level buying clothes in such a store as she eventually did about buying books in a bookstore. Bella became a devotee of thrift shops as well as of Tiffany. And when items from both were put together on her person at the same time, the look sometimes added up to something odd. Of course, that oddness could be used to gain attention, particularly if it might help her land a job such as the one she got with the Campfire Girls by dressing up like her idea of fire and the woods.

While in her real life, she may have had personal conflicts about spending money on clothing and things, she used descriptions in *Streets* of physical settings and clothing with skillful deliberateness. She was acutely aware of the significance of all things visual. In the Prologue, Bella says, "A rabbi divorced my mother from my father, 'since God so willed.' Then my mother bought me a red dress and got passage on a ship for America called Fiume." The red dress was used as an upbeat symbol.

Bella's ever-present money worries took on even greater significance when her mother's eventual marriage to "the pants presser" failed. And Bella was sure from the start that it would. Of all the leading characters in *Streets*, Bella's stepfather, Noosan, was consistently seen by her as a loser. She distrusted the relationship between Noosan and her mother from the start.

But the marriage did provide her with one of the greatest loves of her early life, her half-brother, Herschey.

By far, the most dear creature to Bella was that child, so afflicted a few months after his birth with some unnamed, life-threatening illness. Perhaps someone in medical science today could have diagnosed Herschey properly and saved his life. But at the time, probably about 1911 or '12, and with the family's financial circumstances terribly straitened, the child's medical care was hopelessly inadequate.

The anguish Bella experienced as she desperately offered her little brother all the comfort and care that she could is wrenching. It was made more painful by the response of her stepfather. He jeered at her mother, implying that her own little girl may not have been legitimate. And, therefore, there was the underlying suspicion that somehow Herschey was ill because Bella's mother was not a "virtuous" woman (79). Bella internalized his questioning of her possible illegitimacy. The hated Noosan may have been the source of her own doubts about her mother's first marriage. At this point, his only pity was for himself. He cared nothing for Bella. As she says, "He wept at the top of his voice. 'Oh, what have you done to my son?'" (80).

Whether she felt equipped for the job or not, Bella became a full-fledged "little mother" (80). Darkness descended. Her stepfather not only harangued her mother, but fixed her with the same "jeering stare" (80). Inevitably, the day came when Noosan "left us with the jauntiest smile he had ever worn" (80). They never saw him again.

The most dramatic and difficult period of Bella's life was about to begin as she, her mother, and her sickly little brother moved to Goerck Street. As she describes it, with every move they were brought closer to the East River; this time, just two blocks away. If *Streets* offers us any insight into the overwhelming odds so many of our forbears struggled with as they tried to make a place for themselves in this country, the full force of their efforts becomes plain as we peer, with Bella, into the abyss of that frightening neighborhood. "When will this all end?" she asked. "God, if there is a God, when will it end?" (83).

"The chains tightened," Bella said, "on Goerck Street" (82). But there really never was any giving up for her. In the midst of all her fears, tiny Bella not only persevered for herself and family, she went to bat for her school friend, Celia. The Yiddish word, "chutzpah" must have been invented for just such a scene as Bella staged in attempting to stand up to Celia's parents. The girls had completed junior high school, and Bella knew that she was going to go on to high school, come hell or high water. Her mother was determined, too. She was going to be a lady. But Celia's Russian-Jewish family, with a flock of children to support, were in no mood to let Celia waste her time in high school when she could be out working and bringing in three dollars a week.

Significantly, this frustrating battle with Celia's father left a lasting impression on Bella. Celia failed to gain her parents' permission to go on to get a better education. But, Bella remembered, and when she earned enough money, she established the New York Girls' Scholarship Fund (1939) for girls like Celia so that they could, at least, finish high school. At the time, Bella would not have called herself a feminist, but she knew that girls were more likely to be discriminated against both by their own families and the education establishment, and that was unfair. There was nothing that angered Bella more than to see girls with good brains wasting them on three-dollar-a-week jobs. Even as a teenager, Bella knew that with an education a girl could, and should, aim higher. One sad fact about Bella's love of education was her own failure to get a scholarship to go to college. Her formal education ended with her graduation from Washington Irving High School.

The pants presser stepfather was gone, but another child would soon be born. Fanny thought Noosan had left because he was afraid the second child would be sickly like the first. He was very wrong. Daniel Lang, a healthy boy, was born on Decoration Day, 1913. Bella was not yet fourteen years old.

It is interesting to note that Danny, like his sister, became a prize-winning author. With Bella's encouragement and support, Danny attended and graduated from the University of Wisconsin. He was a wartime correspondent in North Africa, Italy, and France, and had a forty-year career as a staff writer for *The New Yorker*. Albert Einstein wrote the foreword to his first book, *Early Tales of the Atomic Age* (1948). Perhaps his best known book, for which he received the Sidney Hillman Foundation Award, was *Casualties of War* (1969). Danny died in 1981.

All of this was much in the future. The reality at the time was coping with one more baby and no money coming in. Bella and her family had to turn to charity. If *Streets* has any lesson for our times, it comes from Bella's skill in communicating the incalculable damage that is done when the giving of charity is as much directed toward humiliating the recipients as in relieving their suffering. She was ashamed of having to appear in person to be judged a suitable candidate for charity. She was quick to observe how cunning and obsequious others were in applying for assistance, but that was hardly her style.

Bella and her mother worked at every job they could find. But they earned woefully little and if it hadn't been for the private charities, they could not have paid their rent. Had there been a social welfare program at the time, they might have been able to sustain themselves and even have saved the ever-so-slowly fading Herschey. Bella's factory work, baby sitting, tutoring, and all of the other jobs she undertook brought her enriching experiences, but barely enough money to allow her to stay in school. But, somehow, she hung on.

The greatest boon to them all was getting jobs that took them to the country—the Catskills. They were lucky enough, at different times, to find menial work there. It's hard to imagine Bella, who was less than five feet tall, carrying a heavy soup tureen, much less trays laden with food. But, she did it. What isn't hard to imagine is Bella admitting to an error, having on one occasion disturbed the belongings of a child in the boys' school where she worked. When the boy had the audacity to call her "the maid," that was too much. "I'm not a maid," she cried out. "I'm not a maid. Don't you dare call me that." Evidently, the boy and the school's counselor were astonished. As Bella said, "One of the maids had acquired identification" (151). To be sure, Bella did not know what she would become, but she knew she wasn't destined to be a servant. It's just as well. Bella claimed a certain prowess at scrubbing pots and shining windows. But if Bella never thought her mother had a natural talent for dressmaking, Bella was no accomplished housekeeper. She had other gifts.

On her return from one summer's stint of working in the country, she came back to a truly deplorable situation. Her mother was an unrecognizable drudge; Danny, although well grown, looked "pale and fagged out"; but her dear Herschey's face was partially paralyzed (152).

Life dragged on, with school her only real oasis. When graduation day came, Bella remembered it as "vaguely sorrow-ful" (154). She had already begun her search for work. What she most wanted to do was to write on a newspaper. What she found was a job for two and a half dollars a week as a typist and office girl, and her boss paid for her stenographic tuition. Typical of Bella, she continued to pursue her dream to become a reporter. And she met with success. She went to the Yorkville paper, told the editor "I can write," and was hired at space rates, three dollars a column (155). She was on her way.

But one overwhelming sadness was still to come. Just as Bella felt herself gaining ground, her hopes rising, Herschey died. It is impossible to measure the depth of Bella's grief. She never had children. She did assume responsibility for Danny's education, and, in time, for the care of her mother. In a way, it may have been the memory of Herschey that caused her to undertake, with Sam, the founding of the facility now called the Ilan Sport Center for the Disabled, in Ramat-Gan, Israel.

If there are paradoxes in the way Bella lived her life, pieces of the puzzle that don't always come together, there are certain core attributes that were there from the beginning. It is easy to hear Bella saying, "I can write." Her belief in herself as a writer was unshakable. And she did not hesitate to place a monetary value on her skills. She told the tale of bearding a prominent Hollywood producer at a party who had failed to pay for work she had done. He was both famous and powerful, but she had fulfilled her part of a bargain they had made and she had no compunctions about demanding her due, and she got it. That kind of forthrightness was her hallmark.

One trait of Bella's that could be difficult to cope with was her constant fear of poverty. She never recovered from the deprivations she suffered as a child. In truth, she never understood that her success, for which she had struggled so valiantly, had brought her financial security. It did not matter that she had a long list of famous friends; that she could travel to Mexico with the great composer Stravinsky; that she and Sam wrote stunningly successful movies like *My Favorite Wife* or *Weekend at the Waldorf;* that they collaborated on two musicals with Cole Porter, one of which, *Kiss Me, Kate,* won a Tony Award. None of that ever freed her from her memories of being poor. And while she could write an impressive check for a charity, she couldn't leave an electric light on when she momentarily left a room. The wolf was forever at her door.

However, poverty never crippled Bella's imagination nor her creative ability. It may even have driven her to the typewriter when she should have felt free to take time off to relax and enjoy her successes. Her writing career, for the most part, came to a close with Sam's death in 1971. She continued to travel and enjoyed seeing her plays produced in different corners of the world, but her work was largely done.

Bella's life began in hardship. In *Streets,* she paints a multifaceted picture of a tumultuous time. Through it all, Bella's courage never deserted her. She wanted to have her say, and she did.

The Helen Rose Scheuer Jewish Women's Series

Streets: A Memoir of the Lower East Side
by Bella Spewack

The Maimie Papers: Letters of an Ex-Prostitute
by Maimie Pinzer
edited by Ruth Rosen and Sue Davidson

A Cross and a Star: Memoirs of a Jewish Girl in Chile
by Marjorie Agosín

Apples from the Desert: Selected Stories
by Savyon Liebrecht

*Always from Somewhere Else: A Memoir of My Chilean
Jewish Father*
by Marjorie Agosín

*The House of Memory: Stories by Jewish Women Writers
of Latin America*
edited by Marjorie Agosín

*The Defiant Muse: Hebrew Feminist Poems from Antiquity to the
Present, A Bilingual Anthology*
edited by Shirley Kaufman, Galit Hasan-Rokem,
and Tamar S. Hess

REDISCOVERED CLASSICS OF AMERICAN WOMEN'S WRITING
from the Feminist Press at The City University of New York

A Brighter Coming Day: A Frances Ellen Watkins Harper Reader edited by Frances Smith Foster. $14.95 paper.
Brown Girl, Brownstones (1959) by Paule Marshall. $10.95 paper.
Daddy Was a Number Runner (1970) by Louise Meriwether. $10.95 paper.
Daughter of Earth (1929) by Agnes Smedley $14.95 paper.
Doctor Zay (1882) by Elizabeth Stuart Phelps. $8.95 paper.
Fettered for Life (1874) by Lillie Devereux Blake. $18.95 paper. $45.00 cloth.
The Little Locksmith: A Memoir (1943) by Katharine Butler Hathaway. $14.95 paper. $35.00 cloth.
I Love Myself When I Am Laughing . . . and Then Again When I Am Looking Mean and Impressive: A Zora Neale Hurston Reader edited by Alice Walker. $14.95 paper.
Life in the Iron Mills and Other Stories (1861) by Rebecca Harding Davis. $10.95 paper.
The Living Is Easy (1948) by Dorothy West. $14.95 paper.
The Maimie Papers: Letters from an Ex-Prostitute by Maimie Pinzer edited by Ruth Rosen and Sue Davidson. $19.95 paper.
Not So Quiet . . . Stepdaughters of War (1930) by Helen Zenna Smith. $11.95 paper. $35.00 cloth.
Now in November (1934) by Josephine W. Johnson. $10.95 paper. $29.95 cloth.
This Child's Gonna Live (1969) by Sarah E. Wright. $10.95 paper.
The Unpossessed (1934) by Tess Slesinger. $16.95 paper.
Unpunished: A Mystery (1929) by Charlotte Perkins Gilman. $10.95 paper. $18.95 jacketed hardcover.
Weeds (1923) by Edith Summers Kelley. $15.95 paper.
The Wide, Wide World (1850) by Susan Warner. $19.95 paper. $35.00 cloth.
The Yellow Wall-Paper (1892) by Charlotte Perkins Gilman. $5.95 paper.

To receive a free catalog of The Feminist Press's 180 titles, call or write The Feminist Press at The City University of New York, 365 Fifth Avenue, New York, NY 10016; phone: (212) 817-7920; fax: (212) 987-4008; www.feministpress.org. Feminist Press books are available at bookstores or can be ordered directly. Send check or money order (in U.S. dollars drawn on a U.S. bank) payable to The Feminist Press. Please add $4.00 shipping and handling for the first book and $1.00 for each additional book. VISA, Mastercard, and American Express are accepted for telephone orders. Prices subject to change.